WEALTH
Secrets

A WOMAN'S
GUIDE TO OWN
AND SECURE YOUR
FINANCIAL
FUTURE

DEBORAH OWENS

Re think

First published in Great Britain in 2023 by Rethink Press (www.rethinkpress.com)

This book is dedicated to the ambitious, insightful and generous women who shared their unvarnished purse stories in order to help others escape from the middle-class mindset and learn the truth about wealth

Contents

Introduction

Wealthy people have more money than you do; it's true. However, that's not because they're smarter, more talented, or better educated than you are. Wealthy people got that way because they had the privilege of access to the right information. That's the difference maker. Whether from family and friends, acquaintances and colleagues, or intensive self-study, they learned the secrets to building wealth.

If you're a woman who was raised in a middle-class family or was taught to strive for the security of middle-class status, there's little to no chance that your formal education instructed you in the ways of wealth building. Women in America learn all kinds of skills we hope will help us earn more money, but no one teaches us the how-to behind the systematic accumulation of assets. Those of us who don't grow up around wealth find the concept elusive, and that which is unfamiliar to us generally makes us feel uncomfortable.

If the idea of wealth feels foreign to you – like it belongs to someone else – that's understandable. In our society, there are relatively few institutions or organizations designed to help you learn about the subject. In fact, much of this information has for decades been the domain of (predominantly white) men. As a woman, you've likely been taught to pursue higher education, slowly climb the corporate ladder, and save money to create a life of stability and relative comfort. Unfortunately, diligently following those steps won't get you the level of financial independence you so deeply desire.

Like most people – perhaps like you – I wasn't exposed to the fundamentals of wealth building as a child, as a teenager, or as a young adult. I grew up in Detroit at a time when a high school dropout could find a job in a factory and earn enough income to become solidly middle class. My father was an airline baggage handler, and my mother had one of those factory jobs. As their earnings increased over the course of their careers, our lifestyle improved. We moved to better and better neighborhoods. My parents enrolled me at a private Catholic high school, and we enjoyed family vacations.

When my parents retired, they each had a small pension, also known as a defined benefit plan, but no savings or investments. In my family, we always focused on income – specifically, income earned from working.

There was no talk of the value of saving, and there were certainly no conversations about investing to accumulate wealth. After my parents separated, my mother lived on her small pension, Social Security payments, and very little support from my father. At twenty years old, I dropped out of college to earn money in order to take care of myself and not be dependent on anyone. Soon after, it wasn't unusual for me to work sixteen-hour days in my job managing a women's clothing store.

It didn't take me long to figure out I could never work enough hours to create wealth. I realized I might be able to pay my bills and buy nice clothes, but I wouldn't own anything of true value. One day, a chance remark by my mother, "You're always working on holidays. You need to get a nine-to-five job," hit home. This was one of the first times in my adult life that I listened to and acted on her advice. Her comment was the catalyst for me gaining the qualifications for my first job in financial services.

I'd been the first in my family to go to college but had left without graduating. Now, with my new-found determination, I returned to college to gain my degree, followed by an advanced degree. While both these accomplishments were meaningful and valuable, neither helped me learn to invest or to create lasting financial abundance. That knowledge came through my personal study and through my work in a wealth management company.

I started my career in the world of investments as a receptionist at Merrill Lynch, the investment management and wealth management company. I didn't care that the receptionist job was considered a low-level position. I had my sights set on the big picture and what I could learn by immersing myself in the culture of wealth. At the time, I understood very little about investments or how financial markets worked, but it was in that entry-level job, that I had my big "aha" moment.

As a receptionist, I was responsible for answering phones and directing callers to their assigned account executives. This was in the pre-internet world, before clients could access stock prices on their smartphones twenty-four hours a day, so I also gave clients quotes on how specific stocks were trading, which revealed a clear trend. Most of the companies in which the clients held stock were household names such as General Motors, Ford, Procter & Gamble, and Coca-Cola. With caller after caller, I realized wealthy people purchased stock in the companies that made the products bought by middle-income people. Aha!

The people with real wealth weren't just workers and consumers – they owned their own businesses or invested in companies through the financial markets. Business owners used tax-advantaged strategies that allowed them to deduct expenses and have their income taxed at a lower rate. Stock market investors who bought ownership in existing companies saw their money grow at a higher rate of return than it could in a savings account or other low-interest accounts.

The more I learned about the investment marketplace, the more clearly I could see it was just like any other marketplace, and not nearly as complicated as I'd believed. The main obstacle to understanding it was that the people on the inside *wanted* it to appear mysterious and difficult. That way, those on the outside felt they needed a go-between to handle their investing for them, or they'd give up on the idea of investing altogether.

I read *The Wall Street Journal* and built my financial vocabulary. It wasn't long before the branch manager recognized my growth and suggested I train as a registered sales assistant, and I agreed. I studied during every free moment, and I passed the grueling Series 7 exam on my first try – an exam with only a 65% pass rate.[1] Shortly thereafter, I was promoted to registered sales assistant.

In my new position, I met a broker named Emmo – the only woman I'd ever met who earned a six-figure salary. Emmo had great presence and led engaging and informative presentations and seminars. She loved to talk about her passion for investing, and on top of her

---

1. NRS, "The Complete Guide to Passing Your Series 7 Exam" (National Regulatory Services, 2017), https://nrs-inc.com/resources /blog/series-7-exam-guide, accessed 5 June 2023

deep knowledge, she was a model of someone who paid it forward. I knew I had to find a way to spend more time with this woman.

I volunteered to work nights without pay in return for Emmo's mentorship, but she refused to let me work for free. Instead, she offered me a position handling paperwork and calling clients, in return for 10% of her commission earnings. I jumped at the opportunity. This additional role supplemented my entry level salary and included something even more valuable: the opportunity to study a successful woman and learn more about investing.

As soon as I'd built up some savings, I started making my own investments, and within a couple of years, I became a financial consultant at Fidelity Investments. Over five years, I moved up the ranks and became a regional sales manager for the West Coast. Over the course of a decade, I worked my way up to vice president and West Coast regional marketing manager. I loved my work, but eventually I needed a change. The investment industry focused on high-net-worth clients – it still does – but I wanted to make investing accessible to people of all income levels.

Through my work, I had gained access to some of the wealthiest people in the country and to a wealth of knowledge about investment opportunities. **Access is everything**, and I made it my mission to provide that for more people. Specifically, **I wanted to help**

women overcome their fear of investing through coaching, accountability, and support. I dreamed about venturing out on my own and introducing the world of investing to groups of people who were underrepresented in the field and, like myself, were first-generation investors. My husband encouraged me to go for it, and the rest is history.

I launched a career as a financial radio host, and my radio show, *Real Money*, aired on an NPR affiliate in Baltimore for two decades. I also founded Owens Media Group, to develop seminars and workshops for nonprofit organizations. It became my mission to demystify the world of investing and make it simple for anyone to understand. I wanted people to have the tools to acquire wealth without having to rely on anyone else, which meant I had to go further than the radio show allowed.

Every day, a woman of color reaches out to a financial services organization. However, because she doesn't have the foundational knowledge of how the financial markets work – or, in many cases, because she doesn't have enough assets – she's pointed to a low-yield investment that will limit her ability to achieve financial security.

In 2017 I launched WealthyU, a financial wellness company created to give women access to information that could historically be obtained only through private wealth managers. I was – and am – determined to make more middle-class millionaires. Since launching WealthyU, I've gained much more insight into how wealth is created. I chose to write this book to share that new knowledge with as many women as possible.

As America's Wealth Coach™, **I transform cautious savers into confident investors.** While my clients sip coffee and listen to CNBC in the morning, they learn exactly what's going on in the stock market, and they watch in real time as their investments make them money. They scroll through their investment portfolios with conviction and ease. **You too can have a similar level of comfort and peace of mind when it comes to your money.**

In the chapters that follow, you'll learn the truth about wealth and the steps you can take to immediately begin to make the shift from an income mindset to an investor mindset. You'll get the information you need to understand investing, and the strategies to develop your action plan and start executing on it. I have used personal, or what I call 'Purse stories', which are the actual experiences of the women in our coaching programs, throughout to demonstrate how strategies have been used in real-life scenarios by clients. By the end of this book, it's my hope that you will have achieved an increased sense of security and be well on your way to living your wealthy life.

1
Making The Shift: Earner To Owner

As young parents, my husband and I were determined to start our son, from the beginning of his life, on a path to investing. When Brandon was born, we therefore invested in a prepaid college tuition program for him. In Michigan, where we lived at the time, the state offered a program that allowed people to pay for tuition based on a projected cost for when the child would be of age to attend college, and we took advantage of that program.

Although my husband, Terry, and I hadn't yet established concrete financial goals, we knew college education was important. Our desire to provide our children with opportunities motivated us, when Brandon was an infant, to borrow $6,000 and buy in to a four-year college education program. That $200 monthly loan payment put a dent in our budget for three years, but by the time Brandon entered preschool, we had funded his four-year college education – what an amazing feeling. Through three years of small actions, we went beyond earning more and actually put our money to work for our family. This was one of several steps we took to elevate our financial position.

New opportunities

Gone are the days when we all aspired only to make it to the middle class. As more and more people realize wealth is available to them, they move beyond what they were once taught was good enough and the best they could hope to achieve. You picked up this book because you want more. Escaping from a middle-class mindset requires you to revamp outmoded beliefs and behaviors. You need to take ownership of the choices that will lead you to personal, professional, and financial success. Settling for life in the middle class won't give you the financial freedom you desire. You can escape the middle class and build a legacy of wealth when you know what to do, and the Wealth Secrets I'll teach you have been tested by the ups and downs of the financial market. The people who stick with the steps I describe in this book always come out on top.

As we look to create wealth, we can't deny the reality that we're living in a new financial normal. This is not our parents' economy. The days of employer-funded pension plans are mostly over. Some of our parents (or perhaps your grandparents, depending on your age) will have worked for one company for thirty years, and when they retired, their pension and Social Security will have given them enough to live on. However, those defined benefit plans have dwindled and are now almost nonexistent. Instead, most full-time employees have access to a 401(k) plan, which requires them to make decisions about how to invest and secure their future. The 403(b) plan is the alternative retirement plan offered by non-profit organizations and some government employers.

According to MarketWatch, "More Americans have a cool $1 million or more in their retirement accounts than ever before."[2] That's good news, but far too many people are being left behind. As they're growing up and moving through educational institutions, few people learn about the financial markets or how to invest. Unlike previous generations, who back in the day could earn upwards of 14% or 15% interest without taking any risk with their money, these days we'll only earn about 2% interest if we try to avoid all risk. That's not

---

2.   P Brandus, "Opinion: More Americans have $1 Million saved for retirement than ever before" (MarketWatch, August 20, 2021), www .marketwatch.com/story/more-americans-have-1-million-saved-for -retirement-than-ever-before-11629478108, accessed April 3, 2023

enough to build the kind of million-dollar retirement account you'll need, especially because you don't have that old pension plan to rely on. The truth is that millionaire status is the new middle class.

Keep in mind that we're also now in the era of the gig economy. Lifetime careers have become the exception, not the rule. These days, it's not unusual to work for many companies over the course of your career. It's also not unusual for workers to be paid as contractors rather than employees and to receive no benefits. Under those circumstances, each person is responsible for setting up their own retirement plan, and most people don't know how to do this. In 2021, 23.9 million people worked as occasional independent workers in the United States – a sharp rise from 12.9 million people in 2017.[3] The number of people working as contractors is expected to continue to rise, which means even fewer people will have access to a 401(k) or 403(b) plan.

In addition, more and more people in the United States are pursuing service-oriented careers – for example, consulting, nursing, teaching, computing – that require a college degree, while fewer and fewer learn trades. There's a cost to acquire all that education. College tuition costs have increased by nearly 260% since 1980. By comparison, the average cost of all consumer items

---

3. M Vaynerman, "What Is The Gig Economy?" (Bluecrew Resources, September 21, 2022), www.bluecrewjobs.com/blog/what-is-the-gig -economy, accessed April 3, 2023

has increased by 120%.[4] We need to expand our definition of education beyond college and include specialty education, trades, skills, and lifelong learning, all of which can cost significantly less than conventional college tuition.

If you have a college degree, congratulations – you've already made your first major investment, possibly without even realizing it. For most people, however, the investment in an expensive college (with the accompanying student loans) no longer pays a sufficient return. That knowledge, unfortunately, is usually a day late and a dollar short for most of us. If you've already invested in a college education – whether you have no student loans or six figures in associated debt – the most important thing you can do for your financial health is to ensure you get the greatest possible return on that investment. This means leveraging any resources your Alma Mater provides – career counseling and coaching, Alumni associations events for networking, all of which will require you to be proactive in order to receive the greatest benefits.

---

4.   A Jackson, "This chart shows how quickly college tuition has skyrocketed since 1980" (Business Insider, July 20, 2015), www.businessinsider.com/this-chart-shows-how-quickly-college-tuition-has-skyrocketed-since-1980-2015-7, accessed April 3, 2023

Middle-class money myths

I founded WealthyU to provide a financial blueprint for women to overcome the systemic barriers that give them an economic disadvantage. When it comes to wealth, women have to play by a different set of rules, and we can't rely on the advice we received from our parents or grandparents. Conventional wisdom does not lead to wealth, least of all for women.

Our children are doomed to repeat our mistakes if we don't confront and debunk the following myths:

- Myth #1: Student loan debt is good debt.

- Myth #2: A corporate career equals financial success.

- Myth #3: The bigger your home, the more wealth you will have.

- Myth #4: Investing in stocks is high risk.

I've started to address some of these myths already, and in the following chapters, I'll completely dismantle them. You'll read stories of real women who've gone through my training and programs and have learned the truths behind all those myths.

Here's a quick overview of ways to turn those myths on their heads.

1. **Be discriminating and strategic when investing in higher education.** Student loan debt is not good debt. Higher education can derail your life, as highlighted in a 2021 Investopedia article,[5] so it shouldn't be obtained by taking on large amounts of debt. You need to negotiate acceptance offers and consider all sources of education funding.

2. **Be enterprising and flexible, and always have multiple streams of income.** I'll show you how to identify your unique value in the marketplace so you can create multiple streams of income. You will need to become an evolving expert and to differentiate yourself in the marketplace. This will attract recruiters and employers and create an enterprise that can assist you in writing off your expenses and paying less income tax.

3. **Approach the purchase of your first home as an investment property, not as a middle-class status symbol.** Women must be discerning about loan terms and acquire assets that generate income, appreciate in value, or both. We must also avoid using our homes as collateral in an attempt to pay off other debt, or to use the money for buying things that don't appreciate

---

5. T Williams, "10 Ways Student Debt Can Derail Your Life" (Investopedia, June 21, 2021), www.investopedia.com/articles /personal-finance/100515/10-ways-student-debt-can-destroy-your -life.asp, accessed April 4, 2023

in value. Buying a large, expensive home with a huge mortgage won't create wealth. However, purchasing real estate as an investment, and unlocking tax-advantaged strategies of depreciation and deduction of expenses, is the Wealth Secret that one-percenters – those whose net worth is in the top 1% of the population – use to lower their tax burden.

4. **Be an investor, not just a saver.** Learn about the financial markets and how to research, analyze, and make sound investment decisions. Savings accounts won't keep up with inflation. Put the power of great companies to work for you instead. Shift from consuming products to sharing in the profits of iconic brands that can provide you with growth and dividend income.

How do women translate their ambition and achievements into real wealth? The key lies not in earning but in *owning*. I'm here to help you make this shift from earner to owner so you can invest confidently and successfully. I'm also focused on coaching more women of color to overcome challenges unique to their situations so they can build their investment portfolio to seven figures and beyond and create generational wealth. This move from middle class to wealth is possible for all women. It simply requires developing a wealth mindset and seizing the opportunity to learn how the financial markets work. It requires access to the secrets the wealthy have for too long kept to themselves.

This work and your success with investing start with changing your attitudes, beliefs, and behaviors – up-leveling your mindset. Through WealthyU and our financial wellness programs, I've helped thousands of women take that first step and then develop their wealth strategy and execute on it. In the following pages, I'll show you examples of real women, just like you, who were able to build seven-figure wealth once they got the right knowledge. You'll see for yourself that investing isn't just for the rich. *Investing is how you get rich.*

Your Wealth Secrets

WealthyU is in the business of helping women, especially women of color, increase their financial acumen and master the art of investing. To that end, I am revealing the secrets of the one-percenters, which I discovered as a wealth management insider. This is the financial success blueprint that leads to true wealth and freedom.

Here are the Wealth Secrets I'll break down for you:

1. Focus on increasing your net worth

2. Find your superpower

3. Increase your financial acumen

4. Develop a goal-focused action plan

5. Recognize problems as opportunities

6. Leverage tech and systems

7. Protect what you build

This is a completely new way of thinking about your ability to create wealth. I'll walk you through the Wealth Secrets, one at a time, chapter by chapter, and you'll see how other women have applied them. To name just a few, you'll meet:

- Tisa, who tapped into her superpower to become a college financing expert and business owner

- Diya, who increased her financial acumen and learned to make her own decisions about where her 401(k) was invested to increase her returns

- Tamika, who created a goal-focused action plan that allowed her to pay off her high student loan debt

For now, here's a brief explanation of the blueprint that will take you from earner to owner.

Wealth Secret #1: Focus on increasing your net worth

The first step in your success blueprint is about learning how to turn your income into wealth, which starts with focusing on increasing your net worth. The following chapters will show you how women have accelerated their financial growth by increasing the amount of money they were contributing to their retirement plans. They also had a significant amount of money invested in the stock market and in stock mutual funds. They made these changes after assessing their net worth and realizing they could intentionally grow it.

Wealth Secret #2: Find your superpower

Your goal should be to save ten times your final annual salary by the time you retire, especially if you don't have a pension plan. To achieve your financial independence, you'll have to earn more so you have more discretionary income to invest. The days of staying with one employer and settling for 3% annual raises are over. If there is no pension at the end of the rainbow, you'll have to hone your skills so you can demand more income and have the ability to create other income streams, independent of your salary.

At thirty-five years old, you would ideally have saved twice the amount of your annual salary. By forty-five or fifty, you need six times your annual income in retirement savings. I understand that a lot of people have nowhere near what they need in their retirement accounts by the time they realize they need to do something different. If that's the case for you, don't panic. The way you close that personal wealth gap is by having the income to contribute fully to your retirement plan as well as a separate investment portfolio. That all begins with you knowing how to create value through your skill set so you can demand the kind of income you deserve.

Wealth Secret #3: Increase your financial acumen

This is about understanding how the financial markets work and truly mastering the art of investing. To truly accelerate your financial growth, you need to put the power of compounding to work and learn how to invest in stocks that have historically returned 10%. This way, your money doubles every seven years – more than four times faster than the average 2% rate. The leap from a couple hundred thousand to a million dollars at retirement comes from making your money compound at higher rates of return. According to Morningstar's Stocks, Bonds, Bills and Inflation research which chronicles the historical performance of different assets classes, the only investments that have been able to do this consistently are stocks and stock mutual funds.[6]

Wealth Secret #4: Develop a goal-focused action plan

A goal is a dream with a timeline. A timeline also helps you understand how much risk you can take. To build a portfolio that makes the most of your time and money, you must take calculated risks. You determine how much risk you can take, based on how soon you'll need the money. In other words, when you build an emergency fund, you save it in a lower-risk account because

---

6.   R Ibbotson, *SBBI® Yearbook* (KROLL, 2023), www.kroll.com/en/cost -of-capital/stocks-bonds-bills-inflation-sbbi-yearbook, accessed April 25, 2023

you might need to access it at any moment – a short time frame equals a low risk level. However, if you're putting money into a retirement account and looking to retire in thirty years, you can put your money into moderate to high-risk investments and accounts. Your action plan will take all of this into consideration.

Wealth Secret #5: Recognize problems as opportunities

That leads us to the most important aspect of building wealth: understanding how to make the most of the times when the market is down. Many people miss out on wealth-building opportunities because they panic when the market gets volatile and their favorite stock takes a dip, moving their money to low-risk investments because they're afraid to lose money. Wealthy people, however, take a different approach. They look for opportunities where everyone else sees problems, and they take full advantage of those opportunities. I'll show you how and why wealthy people do this, and I'll give you specific guidelines to determine how to balance your portfolio, based on your age-related risk tolerance.

Wealth Secret #6: Leverage tech and systems

I'll show you how to use the technology available on your smartphone to establish an investment account for each of your goals. These goals may include cash reserves, college savings, a down payment for your second home, retirement, and alternative investments like real estate, digital assets, or your own business. Some of these are short-term goals, and others are long-term. Each has an accompanying risk level that will help you determine how to divvy up your investments.

Wealth Secret #7: Protect what you build

Escape from the middle-class mindset means you've made it from earner to owner by adopting a wealth mindset. You now own assets that create a family legacy you can pass down through generations. For that legacy to live on, you need to protect it through an estate plan. I'm sure you've heard the horror stories about celebrities like Prince and Chadwick Boseman, who died without a will. This resulted in their assets going into probate and racking up significant legal fees. Estate planning is a critical part of wealth creation and management. I'll show you how to start protecting your legacy right now, where you are, and how to expand that protection as you grow your assets.

This first chapter has introduced one of the most important points you need to know, that student loan debt is not good debt. The following chapters will illustrate this further as well as ways you can avoid or escape your own student loans. I've introduced other key facts, including that a corporate career doesn't create true financial success, a large home doesn't equal wealth, and savings accounts have limited purpose. I've given an overview of the seven Wealth Secrets, which will be covered in detail in Chapters 3 to 9. Before those chapters, I'm going to ask you to reconsider the American dream.

2

How The American Dream Became A Nightmare

For decades, the formula for financial success – allied with the American dream – was simple: college, career, house, pension. Those people who followed the formula found themselves safely positioned in the middle class, living a comfortable life.

The problem? This formula is a lie. It doesn't work and was never designed to allow you to achieve real financial independence. The wealthy and one-percenters know this, while most people don't.

College degrees do not guarantee six-figure incomes, and a six-figure salary doesn't guarantee wealth. Lifetime careers are few and far between, and don't be fooled by the upswing in home prices during the pandemic – houses do not always increase in value. Pensions are now the exception, not the rule. No part of what you've been told about how to secure your financial future is what it once seemed.

Purse story: Remodeling the American dream

Dr Stacey McCoy believed the myth that more education automatically yields more wealth, and she took the same path so many middle-class women take in pursuit of the American dream and its promise of financial success. Without taking on any debt, Stacey got her undergraduate degree and her master's degree – both in chemistry – from Clark Atlanta University. Then she turned her attention to pharmacy school for a doctorate, for which she did borrow money. The program took four years to complete, during which time Stacey worked as an intern at a small drug store, earning just $12 to $14 an hour. She didn't think about her student loans or how she would pay them off. Instead, she focused on the stepping stones to her true goal: a six-figure income.

"I knew I would be making six figures, and as people of color, most of us don't have anybody in our families making six figures," Stacey said, "and so we have always been told that was a lot of money. Like you could do so much if you could just get to that point.

And that's what I wanted to do. I just needed to get there, however I got there."

Common misconceptions

Stacey wasn't alone in her belief that a salary of $100,000 would give her financial freedom. Early in my career, I also bought into the idea that wealth would automatically follow if I crossed that six-figure threshold. Decades ago, our culture arbitrarily set an annual salary of $100,000 as a standard of success, and that number is still quoted, even though the cost of living has consistently risen. Due to inflation, an income of $100,000 in the year 2000 is equivalent to about $176,000 in 2023.[7] We're still told our financial worries will be a thing of the past if we can just reach that level of income, but rarely is that the case for anyone. In addition, when you don't know how to manage your money effectively, $100,000 (or even more) can leave you struggling rather than helping you become wealthy.

Once she finished pharmacy school, Stacey went on to a yearlong postdoctoral program in Savannah, Georgia, on which she earned about $35,000. While her salary still didn't match her ambition, it was a small sacrifice to make for one more year before she finally landed her first full-time position and secured the income she had expected. Stacey was making a good living but still

---

7. DollarTimes, www.dollartimes.com/inflation/inflation.php?amount =100000&year=2000, accessed April 4, 2023

had one problem: She had no idea how to manage all that money or the student loan debt she had acquired along the way.

"I hadn't had any counseling about, 'This is your loan; this is how you're going to pay it off; this is how long it's going to take; this is what it's going to look like for you in the future,'" Stacey recalled. "I never really had anyone talk to me about what that would look like and what other sacrifices would need to be made in order to satisfy that debt."

Just six months before she needed to start repaying her student loans, Stacey still thought she had things under control. "I remember signing up for what, at the time, was called a graduated plan," she said. "And that meant, every five to seven years, your payments would increase. I might have started out paying $300 to $400 a month. It wasn't a whole lot. And I just knew that, in time, it would go away." That was the extent of Stacey's plan for her student loan debt: Make six figures, make regular payments, and the debt would magically disappear.

The key to wealth: Owning

For Stacey to move beyond the myths that kept her trapped, and to escape the middle class once and for all, she had to shed conventional wisdom and adopt a new mindset. The time had come for her to go beyond the goal of middle-class comfort and create a legacy of wealth. Key to that change would be understanding that true financial wealth lies not in earning but in owning. Wealthy people have always understood this. The rest of us – those of us who were taught middle class was the best we could hope for – have, without this knowledge, survived but not thrived.

Stacey joined WealthyU and learned how to look more closely at her retirement plans and how she could optimize them to increase the returns she was earning on her investments. This was the beginning of her thinking like an owner. As you make your shift from earner to owner, you'll need to keep in mind that the idea of owning is different today than it used to be. After the housing crash in 2008, we had to face up to the cold, hard fact that the value of our homes, which were supposed to be our biggest assets, was no longer guaranteed to increase. Owning a home doesn't mean what it used to. Many people understand that now, but they don't yet realize that, long before the housing market crashed, many aspects of the personal-economy landscape had begun to change.

The change began nearly thirty years earlier, when employers started transferring the risk of retirement income to their employees without also transferring the ways to manage that risk. Starting in the early 1980s, the 401(k) rapidly replaced the traditional pension. This was a few years after Congress amended the tax code and created a new tax-deferred account to sock away compensation. Companies soon started offering the

401(k) as a way for employees to save for retirement, and it morphed into the primary retirement plan we see today.

Whether you're an employee or a contract worker, a freelancer, gig worker, or business owner, you now have more choices than ever. You have ever more decisions to make, including choosing between options for your health plans and your savings and retirement accounts. With every one of those responsibilities, you'll need to adopt an owner mentality to maximize your investment. It's on you, not your employer, to manage these plans. This is the beginning of your new American dream – transforming yourself from an earner to an owner.

Perseverance pays off

As Stacey discovered, this transformation requires focus. Over time, she would make a little progress with her financial goals and then fall behind, over and over again. It was a painful cycle. Meanwhile, she was living a life of dreams delayed. Her student loans were preventing her from achieving other milestones, like planning for the wedding she wanted, buying a house, and maximizing her opportunities with her retirement accounts. "I needed to figure out whatever happened to those six figures," she said. "And why is this not turning out the way I thought it should?"

Finally, Stacey reached a crossroads. She had to make a choice: pay the school loans or max out her retirement funds. There was no way she could do both. At the time, she had a 401(k), a 403(b), and a 457(b) retirement plan. Those plans helped her save on taxes because she was in a high-income bracket and the plans let her invest pretax income. At the same time, however, her student loan debt continued to creep up as the interest accumulated. Stacey had finished pharmacy school six figures in debt, and that number barely seemed to go down.

"I was making a small dent, but not much," Stacey explained. "Not enough so that it would count, and I would see my balance was still high nineties. And at that point, you're thinking, 'Well, this is a house. Nobody told me I was signing up for a mortgage.' I think if someone had said, 'You're buying a house,' I would have seen this differently."

Stacey decided to max out her retirement investment accounts even before she figured out how she'd pay off her student loans. She knew time was her best tool in making the most of her retirement accounts. However, as this losing battle with her student loan debt dragged on, her anxiety increased. "You literally feel like your chest is tightening, you can't breathe, you can't sleep at night," she said. "You have to find a way out. You don't have that peace of mind, and peace of mind is really priceless... And people who are higher-income earners, who are paying student loans, whether you're paying $300 a month, or eventually I got up to $1,700 a month, we don't get tax breaks for that."

Stacey knew people who paid $3,000 to $4,000 a month on their student loans. Just like her, they'd done all the "right" things in getting a solid education and earning a substantial income. Unfortunately, so much of their income, month after month, went to pay off those loans that they were practically in the same boat as someone who makes a lot less money but doesn't have the student loan debt. When they looked at the bottom line, it was like all that education was for nothing.

Determined to find some relief, Stacey applied for student loan forgiveness. She had gone to work in the public sector and had made her 120 loan payments (a requirement), but like 99% of applicants, she was – without explanation – denied.[8] Not one to give up easily, Stacey applied multiple times, but she was rejected again and again. She couldn't figure out why until she finally got a response to her inquiries. According to their records (which she hadn't been privy to), Stacey had made 119 of the 120 payments before moving from the public to the private sector. She was one payment short of qualifying for the loan forgiveness program.

---

8. K Lobosco, "99% of applicants were rejected from government student loan forgiveness program" (CNN, September 5, 2019), www .cnn.com/2019/09/05/politics/rejection-rates-public-student-loan -forgiveness-fix-trnd/index.html, accessed April 4, 2023

Stacey was told to go back to the public sector for another month, but she had already moved on with her career. Instead of going backward, she took a second, part-time job in the public sector and worked two jobs for a year, including the early part of the COVID-19 pandemic, hoping to ensure she wouldn't be rejected again. She also connected with Dr Tisa Silver Canady, another WealthyU student, who specializes in helping people navigate student loan programs.

In the fall of 2021, the rules for student loan forgiveness were relaxed, and the government advised people to sit back and await updates. Stacey did that for about a month, but finally, she couldn't wait any longer. In November 2021, she filled out the application once again – her sixth or seventh try. About sixty days later, she finally received approval. Not only had she gotten six figures of student loan debt forgiven, but she was also reimbursed every cent she had overpaid.

"Being on the other side, it was definitely worth it," Stacey said of all her effort and tenacity. "Get your documentation together, print out everything you can, work with a professional who can help you execute, and do not give up."

While it can be difficult to figure out how to begin to invest in your retirement or other investment vehicles while you're struggling under the weight of student loans or other debt, it is possible for you. Just as Stacey found a way, you can find a way too. Part of going from earner to owner is taking responsibility for all your past, present, and future financial decisions. Wealth Secrets will teach you how to do that.

Your new American dream

Throughout this book, I'll show you how to take the steps to become a true owner, not just an earner. The steps look something like this:

1. **Reduce your student loan:** Go to the most affordable college you can with the understanding that student loan debt is not good debt. As I've pointed out, higher education no longer pays a huge return in increased income, so it doesn't make sense to go deeply into debt to get that education.

2. **Adopt a flexible approach to income:** As an owner in the marketplace, you must be enterprising and flexible and always have multiple streams of income. Since lifetime careers are now few and far between, you'll need to become an evolving expert and differentiate yourself to create value.

3. **Invest in real estate:** Through my work with many high-net-worth individuals, I learned the many tax-advantaged benefits of owning real estate. This isn't about a large home for yourself. It's about purchasing real estate as an investment

and unlocking tax-advantaged strategies of depreciation and deduction of expenses.

4. **Become an investor in the financial markets:** Learn how to research, analyze, and make sound investment decisions rather than relying on someone else's judgment. Savings accounts don't keep up with inflation, so you can't depend on them for your long-term goals. Instead, put the power of great companies to work for you. Shift from simply consuming your favorite brands' products to sharing in their profits.

5. **Maintain an emergency fund:** You need cash on hand, especially if you are among the one-third of American workers who participate in the gig economy, which offers little to no benefits. Although gig work is typically flexible regarding hours and location, it also creates uncertainty, and having a cash reserve is now essential. Even if you have a conventional job with full benefits, an emergency fund can protect you from taking on unnecessary debt when life throws unexpected expenses at you.

In today's economy, individuals must assume so much more responsibility than previous generations for their finances. Instead of guaranteed paychecks, many trained and educated professionals are turning to contract work, which can be lucrative but can also translate into more risk. Record keeping and accountability, and responsibility for health benefits and retirement savings, are all on the contractor. Professionals moving into contract work need to be more educated than ever on a range of topics beyond their job description. In fact, we all do.

The perils of student loans

At the end of this chapter, I need to come back to the issue of student loan debt, which is so clearly illustrated by Stacey's story. Mortgages are no longer the only large debt to be concerned about, and for an increasing number of people, a mortgage won't be their first massive loan.

Part of the old American dream we were sold is the idea that higher education – especially graduate school – would position us for career success and personal wealth. It's why Stacey felt comfortable taking on massive student loans to get the degrees required to enter her chosen profession. With the rising cost of tuition, however, most students attending colleges and universities have little choice but to borrow, just as Stacey did for her doctorate degree. Unfortunately, with the exception of a few specialties, higher education doesn't necessarily equal higher income. Student loan debt is not good debt, but if you've already acquired it, I'll show you how to make eliminating that debt a part of your plan.

While many professions require an advanced degree, too many women come out of both undergraduate and graduate school with enormous amounts of student loan debt. Approximately 66% of all American student loan debt is held by women, but female holders of bachelor's degrees can expect to earn only about 81% of what their male counterparts will earn.[9] That's a problem. In addition, graduate-degree-holding Black women like Stacey owe an average of $75,000.[10] Many of those women go to work in the public sector, where salaries are often lower, hoping their student loans will eventually be forgiven.

In truth, for the first few years after the public student loan forgiveness program was introduced, most applicants were rejected, just like Stacey was. Let that sink in. Tens of thousands of people who were expecting their loans to be forgiven learned they'd have to keep making those monthly payments. You may have been one of them.

While that figure improved with the new student loan forgiveness changes, those changes are temporary. There's no guarantee student loan forgiveness won't revert to that same old inaccessibility. It's impossible to predict what new rules the government will or won't place around the program in the future, and even if

---

9. "Deeper in Debt: Women & Student Loans," AAUW (American Association of University Women, August 26, 2021), www.aauw.org/resources/research/deeper-in-debt, accessed April 5, 2023

10. A Johnson Hess, "Black women owe 22% more in student debt than white women, on average" (CNBC, June 14, 2021), www.cnbc.com/2021/06/14/black-women-owe-22percent-more-in-student-debt-then-white-women-on-average.html, accessed April 5, 2023

you've been told by well-meaning school adminis-
trators that you'll qualify, you just can't count on that.
Even more troubling, many people take out private
loans for student loan consolidation. Unfortunately,
what seems like a way to simplify your debts could
be detrimental in the long run. With private loans,
you often pay more interest. You also give up any
federal loan benefits, like forbearance in case of a job
loss, income-driven repayment plans, and yes – any
potential for loan forgiveness, however slight that
potential may be.

Stacey's story highlights the myths of the old American
dream and the importance of understanding and then
optimizing your situation. She realized she would
never achieve her financial goals if she kept managing
her situation the same way. Instead, she found a way
to get out of the student loan debt she'd taken on in
her pursuit of a six-figure salary, and she increased
her income at the same time. She learned what she
needed to know, and then she took action. As Stacey
realized, knowledge is not power. *Knowledge correctly
applied is power*.

Now you know the truth about the American dream,
you can reinvent it for yourself. It doesn't matter if
you've made some mistakes along the way because
you believed what you were told. Just like Stacey and
so many other women I connect with in WealthyU,
you can course correct and get started on your path
to true wealth at any point. In the next chapter you'll

take the first step by embracing Wealth Secret #1 and starting your shift from earner to owner by focusing on your net worth.

3
Wealth Secret #1: Focus On Increasing Your Net Worth

Now that you understand how the financial landscape has changed, it's time to adopt the new formula for success. Your first step in doing so: *Focus on increasing your net worth*. In this chapter you'll explore what wealth means to you (your wealth mindset), clarify your vision, establish your starting point and a timeline, and learn how to make the shift from an income mindset to a wealth mindset. All of this will help you turn your focus from increasing your income to increasing your net worth.

As a part of this process, I'll introduce you to a powerful exercise, called The Sum of Your Values, which

I conduct with my wealth-coaching clients. Wealth is about so much more than money, but only you can define what it means to you. This exercise will help you do just that.

Purse story: Re-educating yourself about wealth

Like so many of us, Dr Sharon Deans built her career by pursuing more education, expecting those degrees to translate into more money, more security, and more freedom. A native New Yorker, she grew up in a single-parent, three-child household in the inner city, and her family experienced a lot of financial struggles. Sharon wanted to avoid that kind of hardship in her adult life, and she believed that if she went to school and got advanced degrees, she would escape the poverty trap. Instead, after earning a medical degree and two additional graduate degrees, she wound up with a staggering amount of student loan debt.

Sharon was the first person in her family to go to college, and although she became a physician, earning a multiple-six-figure income, she was surprised to find herself right where she didn't want to be: struggling. Part of the problem was her desire to help other people as much as possible – something many of us take pride in doing once we reach a certain income level. Sharon joked that, with her new income, she became the First

National Bank of Sharon to her family. It was exciting, in the beginning, to have enough money to help, but Sharon found it difficult to say no, and her financial support of others went too far. Overwhelmed, she also lost track of her own spending – a crucial misstep.

Financial makeover

Sharon's journey to wealth started in 2020, which her vision board had identified as the year she would get her money in order. She began by signing up for my one-week financial makeover challenge, which includes taking a close look at your spending. When she looked at the numbers, Sharon was horrified to see how much money she was wasting.

"When you grow up in poverty, a lot of times it never leaves you," Sharon told me. "I think what we learn as a society is that people wear their wealth. And so you drive the fancy car – which, I give myself credit, I've never done – but you drive the fancy car, you live in the big house, you dress a certain way. And so I was actually a bit caught up in that, but not in an elitist way. It was just a lack of mindfulness, honestly. And then that inner seed of poverty, just displaying that I'm not poor anymore."

Sharon felt she was always trying to make ends meet, and she realized she made far too much money to feel that way – a situation many of the women I coach have experienced. She started educating herself about her relationship with money, which might seem ironic for someone who had also earned an MBA. Contrary to popular belief, however, the typical MBA program doesn't teach much about managing personal finances.

As she learned more about wealth creation, Sharon discovered she still had a middle-class mindset focused on a pursuit of income. Unfortunately, no matter how much she earned, she still didn't know how to turn that income into wealth. Sharon was interested in investing, but mainly she contributed to her 401(k) and then let someone else take care of her other investments. By her own admission, she didn't really know what she was doing with her money. *She didn't yet have an owner mentality.*

While this might all sound like bad news, Sharon was ready to take critical steps on her road to escaping the middle class. Through my program, she learned about investing and how to see money as the tool it is. She continued to work on her mindset and separated her income from her identity. As she did so, she purged a lot of unnecessary items from her life and from her home. Sharon was on her way to creating wealth, and she would let nothing stand in her way.

When her new job took her to a different city, Sharon chose to rent out her previous house, even though she could have paid the two mortgages without the rental income. Instead of letting that home sit empty, she turned it into a tool for wealth generation, bringing her closer to her big-picture goals. She also set a goal to replace her W-2 income with real estate or other income streams, and she did that within a year.

Sharon applied for and was accepted into Amazon's Delivery Service Partner program, where she manages a fleet of vans and a team of employees delivering packages for Amazon. She had tried to get into this program a few years earlier but had her application rejected. Now that her finances were in order, however, she was approved and able to move forward. She also invested in real estate through real estate syndication and a joint venture. Sharon was no longer struggling financially. She was thriving.

Sharon's story is a powerful example of what happens when you switch from an earner mentality to an owner mentality and find ways to increase your net worth, making your income work for you. She started by leveling up her money mindset; then she formed a solid strategy to get out of debt and build wealth; and finally, she followed through and executed her plans. Part of her success with execution was due to her clarity and focus. Sharon was clear that she wanted to invest in real estate and small business, and she identified what that meant for her in each of those areas. This helped her avoid getting distracted by other opportunities.

Your wealth, your values

Your values should be your guideposts as you shift from a focus on income to a focus on your net worth and how to consistently increase it. This requires a few actions on your part:

1. Identify your highest values.

2. Determine what resources you need to actualize those values in your life.

3. Set clear goals and timelines so you can close the gap between where you are right now and where you want to be.

As one of her core values, Sharon wanted to leave a legacy for her children and give them the building blocks to do the same for the next generation. "For me, it's all about legacy," Sharon said. "I have four children and five grandchildren so far, and I want to teach them how to build wealth. And they all have been taught to give back. We all give back on a regular basis, so that's part of their fabric, but to be able to build wealth – it just gives you the freedom to live the way you want to."

However, after all those years of schooling, Sharon found herself mired in debt, which kept her from creating the legacy she envisioned. She earned a high income, but it seemed she was no closer to financial security and success than she had been as a child growing up in the inner city.

In WealthyU, Sharon learned she needed to focus on her values and her vision, and once she did, she also became a great example of what can happen when you get crystal clear about your finances and truly understand your numbers, rather than avoiding them or glossing over them. By working on her mindset and making some adjustments, Sharon quickly shifted from an earner outlook to an owner outlook. She took her net worth out of the negative to multiple hundreds of thousands of dollars – a transformation available to anyone willing to do the work.

To create wealth while also creating the life you desire, your shift from earner to owner must be grounded in your values. Wealth building shouldn't mean betraying your morals or behaving unethically – in fact, like Sharon, you can do well while doing good. When she invests, she looks at how she can help a community and whether there's an opportunity to diversify within that business. She invests in workforce housing, for example, and is proud to report that her Amazon delivery business employs forty-six people. She's exploring how to expand that business, learning more about transportation logistics, which offers plenty of opportunity to diversify her portfolio within that business model.

Sharon also plans to coach other people outside of her family to expand her legacy in new ways. To this end, she trained in executive and leadership coaching, which gave her another income stream. She got a lot more comfortable with investing, stunning her financial advisor one day by speaking up and voicing her educated opinion when she wanted to move some investments around. She also has a self-directed 401(k) and no longer relies on someone else to make those investment decisions for her. Finally, Sharon opened a Stash account and made sure her kids got one too. The personal finance app allows users to buy stocks and other investments, and Sharon wanted the generations following hers to learn at an early age about investing.[11]

Sharon is now a medical executive with location freedom in her job. This allows her to stay at and work from her son's house, and have time with her granddaughters, for three or four months at a time. She continues to work with her children on legacy wealth building and sound money management. Just as Sharon is creating wealth based on her values, so should you. Let's look next at how you can do that.

The Sum of Your Values

One of the first activities I do with my wealth-coaching clients is to walk them through my Sum of Your Values exercise. Instinctively, they know wealth is about so much more than money, and this exercise helps them identify exactly what wealth means to them. Most of my clients share a chief aim of achieving

---

11. C Rakoczy, "Stash Review [2023]: How Does It Work" (FinanceBuzz, April 3, 2023), https://financebuzz.com/ultimate-guide-to-stash, accessed April 5, 2023

their aspirations and creating a life without strife and worry for their loved ones, and I'd be willing to bet you do too. To create that life – which looks different for everyone – you need to identify your values and what's important to you, and align your financial behavior to reflect those values.

Your bank statement provides an accurate accounting report of what you value. Consciously or subconsciously, you spend money on the things and experiences you prioritize. The Sum of Your Values exercise isn't just a fun way to list your dreams and fantasies – it's a crucial activity in defining what you want so that you can get it. Note down all the thoughts and answers in the way that best suits you. You may prefer to work and edit your list on a computer or tablet. If you think more creatively using pen and paper, you might like to download my Sum of Your Values worksheet at www .wealthyu.com/secretsbook.

This exercise is designed to help you get clear about what you need to feel fulfilled. Your list can include anything from loving relationships to financial and physical security, from a spiritual connection to good health, intellectual satisfaction, or whatever you truly desire. Be specific, and write it all down. This will ultimately give you clarity about what you want your life to look like five, ten, and twenty years from now, as you make these values your reality. When you value something and approach it with integrity, the universe will conspire to help you get it.

EXERCISE: SUM OF YOUR VALUES

1. Determine your main goals

The first step in identifying your highest values and your priorities in life is to pinpoint the main problems or goals keeping you up at night. Start by identifying and then prioritizing what will give you the greatest sense of peace and satisfaction.

Some examples:

- Financial security
- Health
- Resources to care for an elderly parent
- Funds to send your children to college without debt
- The chance to finally do work you love
- The ability to pursue a project you've put off for far too long

2. Decide on the ultimate setting

Let's say you could create your perfect financial situation. Think now about where you would like to live while you enjoy that outcome.

Examples:

- A penthouse apartment in the center of Manhattan, within walking distance of your design studio and your favorite restaurants
- A sprawling estate in the countryside, surrounded by lush green fields and the sounds of a babbling brook
- A tropical island, with warm sand under your feet and a frozen cocktail in your hand, the sounds of

> waves crashing on the shore, and a steel drum playing in the distance

- Any combination of those – you would love to own more than one ideal home

3. Plan your route

After you identify what you desire, where you want to go, and what needs are unmet, you can plot the steps to get there. What are some concrete, measurable ways to move forward? List the steps you can take to achieve your goals, for example:

Providing care for an elderly parent

1. Investigate different care options
2. Liaise with your parent and other family members to decide on the ideal option
3. Set a generous budget, allowing for inflation

4. Prioritize your goals

Write down your goals, with a targeted completion date for each, and include the estimated cost for each goal. Don't worry if you don't know how you'll make it all happen yet. We'll dive deeper into your plan in the following chapters.

Determining your starting point

Before you can chart a clear course to where you want to go, you must honestly evaluate where you are. Too many women avoid taking a hard look at their finances and never take the time to figure out their net worth. I understand the reasons for that – this evaluation can be emotional. We attach so much shame to situations where we haven't yet achieved what we think we should have by now. We blame ourselves for wasting time and money. This is a normal reaction, but you don't have to stay stuck there. Just by reading this far in this book and completing the initial exercises, you've taken your first steps toward increasing your wealth. You're actively engaged in improving your financial situation. You should feel proud of that!

Early in her transition to a wealth mindset, Sharon figured out her net worth simply by listing her assets and liabilities and subtracting the smaller number from the larger one. She discovered the result was -$1,500. After she paid off much of her debt to eliminate her liabilities, her net worth increased into the positive, and she looked at how to continue moving that number in the right direction.

Sharon was brave enough to figure out exactly where she stood. How many people do you know who make a good living but have no idea what their bottom line is? The answer is probably higher than you think. They couldn't begin to tell you their net worth, and yet they continue to spend, often racking up debt, hoping their next pay raise or bonus will help them dig out from under it all. Remember: The same habits can only give you the same results, and bad habits with a higher income can translate into bigger trouble.

Now it's your turn. Before you build wealth, you need to know your starting point. It's important for you to put some specific numbers on your financial status, to list your assets and liabilities and know exactly how much money you're earning and exactly where you spend it. This takes a bit of organization, but it's perfectly doable, one step at a time.

EXERCISE: YOUR STARTING POINT

1. **Organize your paperwork:** Do you know where all your financial documents are? If not, it's time to designate a place for them – perhaps a couple of drawers in a file cabinet or a couple of filing boxes. Fill one of those drawers or boxes with papers representing income, and the other with paperwork representing expenses. Next, get a sheet of paper or create a spreadsheet and list all the money going out on one side, and all the money coming in on the other. Total each side and determine whether you have more coming in or going out.

2. **Store digital backups:** In addition to paper copies, you should keep digital copies of your financial paperwork as backups. Organize these documents on your laptop, and back them up to an external drive or to the cloud through a service like Google Drive or iCloud.

3. **Identify your assets and liabilities:** At the top of another sheet of paper or a new spreadsheet, write "Assets" on one side and "Liabilities" on the other. Liabilities are any debts you owe, including student loans, credit card debt, auto loans, personal loans,

taxes, and mortgages. Assets are things you own that have financial value, including real estate, vehicles, stocks, bonds, mutual funds, your savings, and retirement accounts. Note the value of each liability and each asset.

- Some items will go on both lists. For instance, if you own a house, you'll write down what you owe (the mortgage) on the liabilities side and what the house is worth (its resale value) on the assets side.
- When you've written both lists, add up the numbers and find a total for each. This information will give you a good idea of your net worth:

assets – liabilities = net worth

- This can be a positive or a negative number, but don't beat yourself up if the number is nowhere near where you want it to be. (Sharon's was in the negative, but that didn't stop her from building wealth.)

If you're one of the lucky few, you may be happy with the positive number you see when you total your net worth. If so, congratulations – you have a great starting point for your next level of wealth. Most people, however, will see a number far from what they want it to be. If that's the case for you, congratulations to you too – you've faced this head on, and now you can do something about it.

Be aware that shame, anger, and embarrassment can all come up in this process. That's all perfectly normal. Feel those feelings, forgive yourself and anyone else involved, and move on.

Another emotion that often arises during this exercise is fear. You organize your finances and understand you need to change, but you have no idea where to start. You feel like you've tried and failed before, or you worry you'll never make up the gap between where you are and where you want to be. Fear can destroy your ability to create wealth. It can dampen your faith in the possibility that you can create a successful outcome. Fear is the biggest obstacle to investing, and I understand why. Women in particular have been taught that investing is a space for wealthy white men. We've been told it's an extremely complicated process best left to the experts. Few of us learned financial and investing terminology as we grew up, and so it seems confusing. We feel it will take too much time and is far too risky.

My mission is to teach women how to build wealth and to help them understand they can do it. Over the years, I've simplified and shared with hundreds of women the strategies I borrowed from the ultra-rich, allowing these women to make their money work harder and smarter for them. These are the same strategies I'm sharing with you, and it starts with the exercises in this chapter. After you have done this work, you can walk through life with confidence and purpose. You can build an investment portfolio to seven figures and beyond. You can create a legacy of generational wealth.

Connecting your values and your wealth mindset

Before Sharon could dive into increasing her net worth, she had to plug the leaks in her spending. Once she had a handle on the money going out, she turned her attention to strategies to increase her income and then turn her W-2 income into wealth. She started a new job immediately after leaving her old one, so the stock options and compensation that she received from her prior employer, combined with her new paycheck and increased income provided more funds for her to invest, which resulted in her building wealth faster.

After shifting her focus to her net worth, Sharon had the confidence to stand up for herself in new ways. When she underwent a transition at work and left her position, instead of resigning without compensation, she demanded the accrued benefits she was due – and she received them. This helped her reorganize her financial life and position herself to move in a new direction. Sharon was able to pay off debt and become debt-free for the first time in her life. "I tell you, I walked differently," she said. "It was a nice feeling to know you don't have any bills, all your needs are met, and then you have money to be able to invest in yourself and build wealth."

Sharon became more fiscally responsible and aware of what she was doing and where she was headed, and as she learned, she talked to her grown children about mindful living and mindful spending. "A few of them are pretty high earners," she said, "and I don't want them to make the same mistakes that I've made."

As you increase your net worth, like Sharon did, you'll have more money available to invest, as long as you manage it appropriately and in alignment with your values. Not only will those values help you solidify your goals, but they'll also help you determine where to invest your money. It's important to invest in companies in line with your moral and ethical values, which are of course unique to each one of us. Depending on what matters most to you, socially responsible investment firms, companies working to reduce their carbon footprint, or companies that prioritize animal rights might rise to the top of your list. You may want to invest in companies that support social justice issues, are working to slow climate change, or treat their employees exceptionally well. In the past, it was somewhat difficult to find this information about companies. Today, you can find everything you need to know with a little online research.

Enjoying your new mindset

Sharon now sees investment opportunities everywhere. She went from an unsure novice, who was passive with her money, to a woman who calls the shots in her finances and continues to educate herself. Most of all, she can give from a full cup, not a half-empty one.

"I think it shifted my confidence... knowing that I can manage money very, very well," she said. "When I get ready to relocate to the southeast, I have no worries that I'll be able to secure a home. It allows you this confidence when you can command the tool of money – because it's a tool in our society that you have to command well in order to be able to navigate."

As you develop your confidence in your investing skills, I always recommend you invest in companies you understand, which goes hand in hand with investing in companies whose values align with yours. Start paying attention to the products you shop for and are interested in. This will give you clues as to what you understand best and may want to invest in. Then dig into those companies and find out what they stand for and how they function as corporate citizens.

As you go through this process, keep in mind that wealth building is a long-term relationship, not a one-night stand. Only invest money you don't need to access for at least five years. This way, you can ride out the ups and downs in the market, and you stand a better chance of turning a good profit. Building a diversified portfolio over an extended period generally lowers your risk levels.

Your time is also a resource you must invest in your wealth building. Many people think it takes too much time to invest, but is that true? Imagine the potential improvement if you set aside a couple of hours each week to educate yourself and to research opportunities. What if you invested five hours or ten?

Just like money, your time accumulates compound interest. Those couple of hours per week add up, until you've one day gained confidence and taken on significant information. As your knowledge accumulates, you become more efficient, and the time you need to dedicate to investing decreases. Think of what you could accomplish by trading a few Netflix shows a week for research and education. You can still relax and unwind with your favorite programs, but just like you got organized with the flow of your finances, you can do the same with your time.

Choosing to devote some of your time to learning about investing and understanding the opportunities available to you makes the difference between an earner and an owner. When you're an owner, you're always on the lookout for ways to improve your business – you never clock out. This doesn't mean you run yourself ragged. This is about training your mind to remain open to ideas and opportunities. You invest your time as well as your money, understanding that both are vital to your growth and success. The businesses that do best are those with owners who clearly understand their market. That's the kind of owner you want to be.

When you're an earner, you think in terms of ways you can work to bring in money, which might mean searching for a better job or even multiple jobs. While this is important when you need an immediate income boost, on its own, increased income doesn't help you build wealth.

Instead of only looking at how much money you can bring in, you look at how to leverage your money to make more and grow your net worth. Again, this means viewing money as a tool. Stocks and investments are like a business you own (and indeed, a share in a company is part ownership of that company) rather than a paycheck you cash. You decide exactly what goes into your business and how you plan to run it, and you tend to it regularly. There's no such thing as a truly passive business; even the ones that don't require you to physically be there every day still require you to remain educated and updated and make informed decisions.

Just as in your interpersonal and romantic relationships, it's also important to value yourself above all else in this process of increasing your net worth. That self-value will keep you focused on what's most important. When you know your worth, you can finally create wealth for yourself and for your family. You can take ownership of your future and close the gap between where you are and where you want to be.

Wealthy women think of money as a tool to help them achieve what they want. Money is a key you can use to unlock important doors – doors that determine the way you live today and in the future. Wealthy women realize money is the tool that can help them become financially independent and fund the philanthropic endeavors about which they care so deeply. When wealthy women look at their money, they define the best use of that money and how they can use it to make even more money to achieve what they value most.

In this chapter you've nailed down your values, set big-picture goals, and started to create a plan to achieve them. You discovered how those values can inform your investing decisions. In the next chapter, you'll identify the value you have to offer in the marketplace. You'll do this by tapping into your superpower to maximize your income and your investments at the same time. This may sound like a challenge, especially if you've never thought of yourself as having a superpower, but I'll walk you through it.

4
Wealth Secret #2:
Find Your Superpower

You've created your wealthy vision for your big-picture goals. Now it's time to assess the skills, knowledge, and abilities that can help you make those goals a reality. With Wealth Secret #2 – find your super-power – you'll learn to view your skill set as an asset. In the new financial normal, your ability to create wealth will be determined by how you can get the best return on your talent. Rather than solely focusing on a career path, you'll need to position yourself to take advantage of growth opportunities by leveraging your superpower.

Once you identify your unique strength, you can use it – in multiple ways – to create value and differentiate yourself in the marketplace. This will require you to find growth opportunities, including roles and industries, where your asset is in demand. These opportunities will give you a greater return in the form of higher income and valuable relationships. In the best-case scenarios, they will also enhance and expand your competency, preparing you for the next level of your work. Your ability to negotiate a higher salary or rate for your services, by conveying or selling your unique value to others, will be a major determinant of your financial success.

Purse story: Taking control

When Dr Tisa Silver Canady came to work with me as one of my wealth-coaching clients, she had all the degrees and the responsibility, but her income didn't match the value she was providing. She had hit a wall in her career. Like many people, in particular many women, she felt she needed to settle for what she had in her job and could only hope someone would eventually recognize her contribution and she would be promoted.

After a long career in higher education, during which she taught corporate finance and investments, Tisa transitioned into a job as assistant director of financial education and wellness in a financial aid office of a major university in Baltimore, Maryland. There she counseled students about how much to borrow in student loans and how to repay those loans after graduating. Over the years, she helped students and their families pay off more than $50 million in student loan debt, and she felt great doing it.

Tisa recognized she was doing good work. She was making a real difference for the people she served, but the need for her kind of expertise was so great that she felt pulled in multiple directions. In her desire to help, she took on more and more responsibility. After a couple of promotions, she had advanced to the director level, but she no longer felt in touch with the work that had ignited her passion. She appreciated the knowledge she'd acquired about financial aid, registration, and other areas of higher education, but her work no longer felt like the best use of her time and expertise. So many students struggle with student loan debt – a burden they could avoid or drastically reduce if they only knew how. Her role with her employer limited her reach, so Tisa started thinking about what she could do as a personal mission that went beyond one campus.

While she was ready to do something different, Tisa wasn't sure what that would be or how she could get there. At the same time, she had a good job with a decent salary, so she questioned whether she should even consider leaving to do something else. While she assessed her options outside of her job, Tisa also advocated for a pay raise. Asking for more money required her to do more mindset work and some legwork. She evaluated her role and the value she brought to the organization, and she considered the request for a salary increase from her employer's standpoint.

Tisa had taken on a lot of extra work, but by her own admission, those tasks weren't in her job description or at her employer's request. She did them because she had a larger vision for her life and for students and families across the state. She therefore had to reconcile the fact that her employer wasn't responsible for paying her for the extra work she'd taken on of her own volition. When she asked for a raise, she left those tasks out of the discussion and lobbied for additional pay based on the work she did that was valuable to the organization. Having made a strong case for the unique value she provided, Tisa received the raise she requested.

Find your comparative advantage

Your superpower is your comparative advantage. It's the skill sets, talents, and body of knowledge that set you apart in your industry or niche. Finding your superpower requires you to identify your strengths and find ways you can use them to create value for others in exchange for income. You will pave your path to financial security by using your gifts and talents to serve others.

Begin by identifying your strengths, which can serve as guideposts to your future wealth. Many women find this difficult to do, for two reasons:

1. We're taught from an early age not to brag, but to remain humble so we don't make other people feel bad with our accomplishments.

2. We're often too close to our own expertise. When something comes naturally to us, we start to feel like it's no big deal and everyone should know how to do it. We take our own skills for granted.

Tap into your superpower

To make the most of your superpower, you must first take on a new belief: *You are not your job*. This is a continuation of the mindset shift you started with Wealth Secret #1, when you shifted your focus from your income to your net worth. Your job is a tool. Even if you went to school for years to learn how to do that job, it does not define you. You're free to choose to do something different for a living.

"I think people, when they hear the calling, when they receive the call for what they're supposed to do, it makes them uncomfortable," Tisa said. "And things happen that make it so that you can't stay in that space of comfort because you know you're not doing exactly what you're supposed to be doing. So I had these feelings. They were somewhat unclear, at first, but over time, I just got to be so uncomfortable, and I didn't know what to do with it."

Tisa and I met because of our work in financial literacy, and she had been a guest several times on my radio show. When she decided she needed help figuring out how to utilize her unique skills to fulfill her purpose, she reached out to me for wealth coaching. This was a critical mindset shift for Tisa. She had been trying to figure everything out on her own, so asking for help was a big step. This was especially important for her because she had never been an entrepreneur and was leaning toward that option as she began to recognize how much value she could offer outside of her current workplace.

The first step I took with Tisa was to help her understand that, by identifying and maximizing her superpower, she could monetize her skill sets beyond her job. You may not yet know what your superpower is, but in this chapter, you'll figure it out. It's also important to realize you can do well and do good at the same time, just as Tisa has done.

Getting more money from her employer was just the beginning for Tisa. I helped her understand that she could also flip her skills into the mission she wanted to pursue, guiding more students and families all over the country and beyond to quickly and wisely eliminate student loan debt. Tisa needed to get paid what she was worth and at the same time make the most of those tasks that fell outside of her job description – tasks that provided great value to her clientele. To this end, I helped her set up informational interviews to learn more about the people in the space she wanted to be in and the work they did. As we lined up the interviews, I included people who had what they considered to be ideal jobs within their organizations.

These interview meetings served multiple purposes. They helped Tisa introduce herself and get a deeper understanding of the needs in her field. They also positioned her with contacts and resources at the ready.

I then had Tisa take the time to investigate different degree programs and look at her finances to see if she could meet her financial obligations if she left her job right away. Based on the numbers, she decided to stay while pursuing her doctorate. One of the benefits of her job was tuition reimbursement, and Tisa maximized that benefit by choosing a program relevant to her line of work – a doctorate in higher education administration with a concentration in community college leadership.

In addition to taking a hard look at her finances, Tisa examined her schedule before going back to school. As a wife and mom with a full-time career, she had to figure out how to make time to study and do the work for her doctoral program, while balancing work and home life. She carved out time wherever she could find it. "It's really about making the decision," she said. "Once you make a decision that this is the direction you're going to go in, I do believe there's power in having a decided heart. So some days, it was late nights. Others, it was early mornings. But once that decision was made, it had to be done."

Keep in mind you don't have to be dissatisfied with your job to tap into your superpower. In fact, you can use your superpower to do something new or to earn more right where you are. When you adopt a wealthy vision, you go deeper with your new wealthy outlook. This might lead to you seeking another job, or it could result in you asking for a promotion, starting a side business, or becoming a full-time business owner.

Think outside the box

In our new economy, many workers have discovered that their jobs do not define them. During the COVID-19 pandemic, millions of people left their jobs, many because they felt underpaid, overworked, and underappreciated. Others had gotten a taste of work life outside of a cubicle, no longer chained to a desk, and they liked it. Rather than go back to getting dressed up for a day at the office and dealing with the hassle of daily roundtrip commutes, they started their own businesses or took on multiple jobs that had more flexibility and allowed them to work remotely. According to the Society for Human Resource Management, four million people per month quit their job in 2021 alone, "the highest average on record."[12] This mass exodus came to be known as the Great Resignation. The pandemic and all that came with it made people reflect on what they wanted in their lives, and some of those people

---

12. SHRM, "Interactive Chart: How Historic Has the Great Resignation Been?" (SHRM, March 9, 2022), www.shrm.org/resourcesandtools /hr-topics/talent-acquisition/pages/interactive-quits-level-by-year .aspx, accessed April 5, 2023

made an essential mindset shift. They realized they had options.

Some who left their jobs during this time made lateral moves, but many created a new wealthy vision for their lives. To make your escape from the middle class, you need the kind of wealthy vision they developed – the same kind of wealthy vision Tisa used to change the trajectory of her financial wellbeing.

The key to thriving in this dynamic economic environment is agility. Once you identify your superpower, you will create a strategy for becoming best in class, by considering questions such as:

- What tools and resources can you leverage?

- Who can be of assistance?

- What can you do to make yourself more valuable?

- What do you need to learn?

- Can you apprentice with someone and trade your time for knowledge?

Tisa had figured out how to see problems as opportunities and to meet the needs of the audience she serves by tapping into her superpower, her unique skills and knowledge in the area of student loan management and repayment. The key to her success was the ability to recognize and take ownership of the value she could bring to any organization.

Since she was unable to find a book on student loan debt for Black borrowers, I encouraged Tisa to write her book *Borrowing While Black*, which explained college costs and how students can make the most of college without mortgaging their future.[13] The book extended her reach, allowing her to serve more people, and further positioning her as the go-to expert in the field.

Tisa now educates members of the community about how to make decisions around investing in higher education, making sure they get a return on investment – just as she did in her own life. Her work is not only creating a positive impact in the Black community that will affect families for generations, but it also allows her to increase her own income to invest in wealth building for her future.

There's no room for modesty – real or false – or for downplaying your gifts in this process. The only way to leverage your strengths to create wealth is to own them. Even if a skill seems common to you, include it on the list in the exercise below. It may be easy for you, and it may even be common in your circle. Invariably, though, many people need help of some kind in any area where you shine.

When Tisa came to me for coaching, one of the first exercises we completed together was my Comparative

---

13. TS Canady, *Borrowing While Black* (Package Your Genius Books, July 29, 2020)

Advantage worksheet, which helped her clarify her superpower and begin to think about how to best leverage it. I'll walk you through that process in the exercise that follows. As you answer the questions, don't hold back for fear of what other people might think. This exercise is for your eyes only, so be completely honest.

EXERCISE: COMPARATIVE ADVANTAGE

Answer the following questions to identify your strengths:

- What specific skills do people compliment you on?
- What do people tend to seek your advice about?
- What are you doing when you lose track of time?
- What is your first memory of feeling a sense of purpose?
- Among all your skills, which have you mastered at a higher level than most people?

If you're struggling to answer those questions, stop here and reach out to a few people who know you well. Choose a colleague and one or two people with whom you have a close personal relationship, and get them to answer the above questions about you. Stay open-minded as you listen to and write down their responses, even if they surprise you, then look for the common threads among all the answers.

If you've participated in a personality or skills profile assessment in the past, you can analyze that information alongside these answers to uncover your gifts.

Where passion and gifts intersect

Because of her new mindset, Tisa was able to ask for help when she needed it, particularly when things felt overwhelming. She put together a strategy, looking at what resources were available to her. Then she executed, sticking to the plan over the years it took to complete her doctoral program – an accomplishment that leveraged her superpower at a higher level, because she was doing work at the intersection of her passion and her gifts.

The doctorate added a layer of credibility to Tisa's resume – an important element in establishing herself in a field where people typically get multiple degrees. Her earlier networking and pursuit of her passion also paid off, as her first contract came from her relationships she'd created through volunteer work. Tisa took full inventory of the financial education and wellness activities happening on campuses across the state. She then set her sights on creating a statewide network with additional infrastructure, to include people in government, corporations, and foundations.

In July 2021 Tisa launched the nonprofit Maryland Center for Collegiate Financial Wellness in a virtual event attended by people from around the country and even Canada. She also founded Silver Canady & Associates, a higher education research and consulting firm. As of June 2022, she has counseled borrowers on their repayment strategies, enabling them to pay off more than $75 million in student loans.

"So what started out for me as an idea in that one office, on that one campus, to reach people across the state, turned into something that resonated with people across the country," Tisa said. "And for me, it's so rewarding to be able to do work that I love, but to also bring people along with me, and to know we're creating a better space for Maryland's college and career students, and even those across the country."

Everything you're good at isn't necessarily something you want to commit your time to doing professionally. You might bake the best German chocolate cake your friends and family have ever eaten, but that doesn't mean you have to own and operate a bakery or start teaching cooking classes, though you could do those things if they align with your desires. Fortunately, you have multiple strengths and can choose those that intersect with your professional passion to tap into as a new source of income. Look over your list of strengths and highlight those you truly enjoy doing, and draw a line through the others.

Once you know where your professional strengths and passions intersect, you've identified your superpower. This is the comparative advantage that will help you succeed in your career or business and increase the investable income you have at your disposal.

You will have taken another step on your road to getting wealthy.

You: A creative enterprise

Albeit an imperfect measurement in some cases, the income you receive through your job, or any products and services you sell, or any business you create, is a measurement of the value you provide. You can use your superpower to boost your income by maximizing that value.

There are three fundamental ways to leverage your superpower to earn more:

1. Increase your job skills

2. Start a side business

3. Take advantage of the on-demand service economy

1. Increase your job skills

If your current career is aligned with your superpower, you can often increase your income without making a major change, simply by increasing your job skills. It doesn't matter if you are a freelancer, a business owner, employed full-time, or all of the above – expanding your skill set makes you more valuable in any role. If you're an employee, those additional skills can position you for a raise in your current position or for a promotion. If you are a freelancer or business owner, your new knowledge can help you streamline your processes and increase your profit margins, or you could add on a whole new line of products or services to increase the bottom line. If your current career isn't aligned with your superpower, you can use your superpower to start a whole new career.

Become an evolving expert. Never stop seeking ways to adapt and innovate, differentiate yourself, and add value. Thriving in the dynamic economic environment we live in requires you to constantly seek to upgrade your skills. Continuous learning is an essential life skill and critical to accelerating your wealth building. Thanks to technology, changes happen faster than ever in almost every industry. A skill set that's valuable today can easily become obsolete tomorrow, leaving you languishing behind colleagues who stay on top of the latest trends. Keep abreast of the changes in your industry, and stay one step ahead by taking on new skills in alignment with those changes.

Don't let the potential cost or time commitment required to upgrade your skills intimidate you. Many companies offer on-site training or tuition reimbursement. Some pay upfront for employees to continue their education through colleges, universities, and other programs. It makes sense to take advantage of this to acquire new skills at no cost to you.

Even if you don't have company benefits to rely on, there are plenty of affordable ways to develop new skills. Online learning is a booming industry, and colleges and universities are coming up with new offerings to compete with independent training programs. Gone are the days when a university program was the only way to get additional skills. Online platforms, like Coursera and LinkedIn Learning, offer professionals almost unlimited opportunities to learn new skills and acquire new knowledge.

2. Start a side business

Starting a side business while you work your nine-to-five job is a great way to test a business idea while you still have a paycheck to rely on. You can also launch a business you plan to maintain as a secondary source of income. How large you want to grow your side business depends on the work you want to do and how much of your resources you're willing to invest.

Your options for starting your side business are limited only by your imagination and what the marketplace desires. Coaching, consulting, tutoring, and online-course creation all provide avenues to create income with your knowledge and experience. In those cases, you might target corporate clients, organizations, institutions, or individuals. If your superpower involves creating physical products, you could start a business selling those products, or you could decide to launch an online course or coaching business teaching people to make that same product. A master jewelry maker might sell her jewelry on Etsy or on her own website, offer classes on jewelry making, or consult with other artists to help them start their own jewelry business. She could also do all three, creating three streams of income with her superpower.

3. Take advantage of the on-demand service economy

The on-demand service economy provides yet another way to use your superpower to create additional income for your wealth-building plan. When you think of on-demand services, you might think of driving for a rideshare company or delivering meals or groceries, but this category encompasses so much more. Even healthcare services can be found on demand, through apps like Doctor on Demand, which opens a whole new area of possible employment for healthcare providers. Other industries with significant and growing on-demand opportunities include logistics, fitness, entertainment, beauty, and home services. Consider what on-demand role might align with your superpower so you can expand your earning potential.

Tisa took her unique combination of experience, knowledge, and wisdom and used it to create value for other people. You can do the same in your area of expertise. Lots of folks may know some of what you know, but you're the only person with your exact combination of skills, knowledge, and passions. Don't underestimate how powerful and effective that combination can be in helping you increase your income, which will give you more money to invest to increase your net worth.

The exercises you've done with Wealth Secret #2 have shown you how your unique gifts, together with your unique blend of innate characteristics and experiences, can position you to achieve the wealth you desire much more quickly. You just have to tap into them and put them to work. In the next chapter, you'll discover how to easily increase your financial acumen. This next Wealth Secret is essential so you can understand how investing works and how to make it work for you.

5
Wealth Secret #3: Increase Your Financial Acumen

Finding your superpower is an important step in making your escape from the middle class and finally getting wealthy. However, as you've seen, earning more money will only help you get wealthy if you know how to put that money to work for you. Unfortunately, many women have fallen into the trap of believing investing is a specialized field they can't master. At best, they surrender the oversight of their portfolios to someone else. At worst, they never even try. If that's how you've felt or what you've done, don't beat yourself up. Investing has been portrayed as the domain of wealthy white men. We've been taught that there's no place for women – much less for Black women and other women of color – in the world of investing. That myth no longer stands up to evidence.

Purse story: Breaking down barriers

Women like my wealth-coaching client Diya Wynn are proving investing for wealth is available to anyone willing to learn the ins and outs of the financial markets. When Diya was growing up, her mother used to say her family didn't talk about money because they didn't have money, so there was no conversation to be had. Like many of us, Diya developed a successful career but had little financial education to go along with it. She had an income mindset and a belief that a good education and a good job were her tickets out of poverty. She didn't think much about her finances beyond putting some money in savings and in a retirement fund. Because she didn't understand investing, she failed to take advantage of other opportunities to grow her money. She needed to learn how to make her money grow.

Back in the "good old" college–career–house–pension days, many middle-class folks could easily afford higher education and real estate. They could confidently rely on their employers to support them to a ripe old age. They could get away with not knowing how to invest and still have the appearance of a comfortable life without having created real wealth. Their pension would cease on their death, and the only asset they would pass on would be their principal residence. The wealthy, on the other hand, have always had investment portfolios, real estate, and trusts that allow their wealth to pass from generation to generation.

I can't stress this point enough. Employers have transferred almost all the risk of financial security in retirement to you, and if you're like most people, you haven't been given the requisite knowledge to manage that risk. What I know from coaching people for years is that not inheriting wealth comes with another disadvantage: the lack of knowledge. When you don't have anyone in your family to show you the tools and resources, you lack the confidence to make investment decisions.

That was the case for Diya. She didn't inherit knowledge of how to create wealth, so she directed her money into whatever program her 401(k) advisors recommended. She chose a target-date fund, meaning she entered her anticipated date of retirement, and then the investment company put a group of funds together based on that date. Diya planned, once she made more money and could invest more, to hire someone to help her maneuver through the process – while she was an expert in her field, she was convinced others knew better when it came to investing.

When Diya joined WealthyU, my group coaching program, where I teach women how to invest and build wealthy habits, she quickly realized she could control more of her assets than she'd previously believed.

When I coach clients, we always start with mindset, and Diya's financial transformation began with the idea that not only could she learn about investing, but it would also be a good use of her time to do so.

"One of the biggest shifts for me was [accepting] I was capable of learning and understanding everything I needed to know in order to be a smart investor, in order to make better decisions that actually allowed me to see a benefit," she said.

Do your homework

Even if you've never invested in the stock market, you can learn what you need to know to make sound decisions and invest wisely. As your level of knowledge about financial markets rises, you'll no longer be afraid of the uncertainty that comes with investing. Once you have this knowledge, you'll never again have to depend solely on any expert's opinion. You'll be able to properly evaluate any advice you get and make your own smart decisions about where to invest your money.

In Diya's one-on-one coaching with me, we started by looking at her retirement funds, and I showed her how to evaluate her returns. She discovered that investments she had considered aggressive were nothing of the sort. Following her advisors' guidance, she was getting limited returns of about 5% – barely any better than a savings account – and we talked about how she could diversify.

Diya went into her investment portal and browsed the other funds available to her, some of which weren't target-date funds but had been getting better returns. She compared what she saw with information she found on the investment research website Morningstar, on Yahoo Finance, and on other sites. She looked at small-cap, medium-cap, and large-cap funds, and also investigated whether to invest in international funds and other areas. This was deeper than she had ever gone in her own research, and once she gathered enough information, Diya made some changes in how her money was allocated. Within the first quarter, she saw some big improvements in her returns.

"I know some of that has to do with what was happening in the market at the time, but some of that shift was really about putting my money in places that were doing better," she said. "And I didn't do that before because I just used what was recommended to me as opposed to evaluating the performance of the fund and understanding what it invests in, and what that means, so I can make better and more informed decisions."

Like Diya did, you'll want to turn to reliable sources for news about how the stock market and specific stocks are doing. Don't allow yourself to get caught up in the hype on social media or in popular media, both of which tend toward exaggeration, when the stock market goes up or down. Always pay attention to the actual numbers, and educate yourself about what they mean.

Most people find funds easier to start with because they spread the risk across many different stocks or bonds. Once Diya had a handle on funds, we turned to stocks. As many people do, Diya found investing in specific stocks an intimidating prospect. She had to wrestle with her belief in herself and the assumption that she didn't or couldn't understand stocks. She also had to face her fear of losing money and her fear of what she considered risk.

I always say you can't save your way to wealth, and Diya took that to heart. She remembered how her grandmother used to keep money under the mattress or in a box in the closet, so Diya understood the importance of saving from an early age. However, she also realized saving alone didn't help her grandmother move out of the projects, and it wouldn't be the vehicle that would help Diya make the changes she wanted to make for herself and her family.

Compound your confidence

As she made more of her own decisions about investing and saw she could successfully maneuver it, Diya gained confidence. She became more curious about other opportunities and started looking into real estate and exploring other avenues for investing her money outside of her 401(k). "I got a little bit more comfortable with investing," she said. "And then I wanted to do it more, and so I'm actively seeking out ways we can grow our income as a family and the things we can do to build that same sort of knowledge and understanding with our children."

Diya had moved from a focus on making more income to a focus on making her income work for her – an income mindset to a wealth mindset. Next came the strategy. After moving out of the target fund in her 401(k) and into a more diversified set of funds, she implemented a system by which she would increase the percentage of her income she invested in her retirement fund by 1% or 1.5%, until she was maxed out. Diya said, "I put in a system so that every year I would increase the percentage that I was actually investing."

As she moved her focus from mutual funds to stocks, she researched specific stocks to invest in. She looked at the items she commonly used and the businesses she supported to see whether any investment opportunities were available in those niches. She also learned how to invest the returns on her stocks into other areas. Then she investigated funds that would allow her to invest in real estate being built.

To find the money for these investments, Diya evaluated where she was spending her money and where she could free up resources, whether that meant personal spending, monthly bills, or things like her insurance plan. She got smarter about her outflow so she could increase what she had available to invest and continue to build wealth.

Now Diya was paying close attention. She had a 401(k) in two places, so she had different institutions in which she could open investment accounts. She opened an account for her son at Sharebuilder – a business that eventually became E-Trade – because she felt that was an easy place to start. She used the platform to start investing with about $500 and then learned her way around stock research. She put a number of stocks on her watchlist and bought them when she was able. One of those stocks was Shopify, and although Diya said she waited a little too long, she still got in early enough to see big increases.

Two things were important in Diya's ability to execute her strategy:

1. She made time to learn

2. She regularly consumed financial information

Previously, she had simply set up her 401(k) and not given it another thought, aside from scanning a monthly or quarterly report that came her way. With a new mindset and strategy in place, she allocated time each week to research stocks, mutual funds, and opportunities. Then she put her plan in writing and created a vision board. She periodically looked at the pictures on the board to figure out the steps it would take to reach those goals.

Join forces

As a first-generation investor, Diya can now pass on her knowledge to her sons and provide them with the tools she didn't have at their ages. They will have the privilege of inheriting the knowledge of wealth creation. Each of her sons has a bank account, and Diya ensures her sons use the register and review their statements with her each month. She talks with them about what to do with money they receive on birthdays and holidays, and they read books and play games related to investing. As a family, they have conversations about topics like income versus expenses, and what liabilities are.

"Those are terms I did not know at all, at eight," Diya said, "but that's a conversation we now have in our home. So we talk about it and help them learn and understand financial considerations they would have to make. We talk about what it requires to buy a car and interest and all that stuff. I didn't know any of those things."

Diya also buys her nieces and nephews stock for their birthdays, along with a toy. She ties the stock to whatever they're interested in – Hasbro stock if it's a Barbie, for example, or Nintendo if they're into video games. "I think we're paying a lot forward in terms of giving them the knowledge and education," she said. "And I think that's going to be invaluable, starting at six or eight versus starting in your forties to understand this."

As Diya discovered, having someone in your corner with whom you can talk through some of your investment decisions is invaluable. When you try to go it alone, it's easy to get caught up in the emotions of the ups and downs of the market. It's easy to take the seemingly safe route and put your money in less aggressive, lower-risk investments. An advisor and a community of investors, both of whom Diya found in WealthyU, can help you make better decisions, even when there are no foolproof guarantees.

Join a circle of like-minded people who have financial aspirations similar to yours. As you develop your financial acumen together, their support can keep you from getting overly fearful and selling at the wrong time. Your peers can help you stay focused and optimize your returns, especially when the market is down and you start to think about pulling out. Learn to live with the ups and downs of the market, and remember to see the opportunities in the downturns.

Start with the basics

Although Diya started off playing it too safe with her investments, she took one important step right from the beginning. *She developed the habit of saving money.* If you don't consistently save a percentage of your income yet, now's the time to start. I don't want anyone to think you'll get wealthy through saving alone – you won't. However, you'll need money to start investing, and the best way you can focus on investments is from being secure in the knowledge that you've topped off your emergency fund and your savings accounts. This is referred to as liquidity – cash you can get your hands on quickly. If you haven't yet built up much liquidity, you might need to cut back on your spending for a while. Don't make the mistake of waiting until you feel you can afford to start saving or to start investing. Time and compound interest are two of your greatest tools to build wealth, so the truth is you can't afford to wait. In the long run, you'll be much better off if you start making small sacrifices to your budget now. Use the money you save to invest and to build your savings at the same time.

Too many people still live paycheck to paycheck or on credit and would be financially devastated by unexpected medical issues or other disasters. You need savings on hand so you're not forced to sell your portfolio – your investments, including stocks, bonds, and mutual funds – at a loss when a financial emergency arises. When you decide to invest your money, you first need to determine your goal. Do you want growth, income, or a combination of the two? This largely depends on how much time you have and how much risk you're willing to take.

When you deposit your money into a savings account, you make a loan to the bank. The bank makes its own investments and pays you a return in the form of interest. This is considered safe because the bank is typically insured by the federal government. However, your money doesn't grow much because the interest you earn doesn't always keep up with inflation. On the other hand, stocks have historically earned an annual rate of return of 10%. Of course, this is an average over time; some years will be better than others.

Time to take stock

Although many experts still make the financial markets seem mysterious, they aren't as complicated as you've been taught to think. It's also an outdated myth that you need a lot of money to get started or that you need to get past a gatekeeper.

Essentially, there are only three ways to make money in the financial markets: growth, income, or a combination of the two. You can invest in bonds that pay interest income, or stocks for growth and/or dividend income. The great news is these types of investments are readily available through:

- **Mutual funds.** These come with professional money managers and low minimum investments.

- **Exchange-traded funds.** These are not actively managed by a fund manager but follow the performance of a particular market index. (A market index tracks the performance of a specific group of stocks or other assets.)

In this age of the 401(k), it's important for everyone to learn about stocks. Traditional pensions offered guaranteed automatic payouts based on a formula that took an employee's salary and number of years of service into account. The longer an employee worked, and the more he or she earned, the higher the payouts would be in retirement – employees didn't have to think about much more than that. Now we all need to have some fundamental financial knowledge. We must make a shift.

This is a truth serum we all need to take. Everything we were taught about achieving financial security was a lie. Social security is barely enough income to survive on, pensions are nearly nonexistent, and traditional savings and fixed income investments have not kept up with inflation.

If you consistently seek and consume financial knowledge, you're guaranteed to learn more than the average American knows about investing. If this feels like an intimidating proposition, remember you don't have to do it alone. Face your fears and share your concerns with your financial advisors, your accountability partners, or your investment community. When you overcome fear and intimidation to immerse yourself in learning about the financial markets, you open yourself up to reap much more of the rewards of investing than you'll likely get when you delegate all your decision making to the experts. Diya did it, and so can you.

Wealth Secret #3 – increase your financial acumen – will position you to escape the middle class by learning the language and fundamentals of investing, which is how the wealthy one-percenters I advised during my career in financial services achieved their lofty status. You'll need to develop an appetite for this knowledge and commit to increasing your financial acumen over time. One of the reasons I created my wealth-coaching business was because the knowledge of how to build wealth is not taught in our formal education. This lack of information makes it difficult for most people to maximize their retirement funds or invest beyond those funds. It's my mission to make sure more women get access to high-net-worth strategies to accelerate their financial growth and achieve the level of financial success they desire and deserve.

All the new financial knowledge you're acquiring as you increase your financial acumen will go a long way to help you with the next Wealth Secret: developing your goal-focused action plan.

6
Wealth Secret #4: Develop A Goal-Focused Action Plan

I t's time to take the next step to make your values, dreams, and aspirations a reality. You've gotten clear on your priorities, and you're beginning to master the basics of how to put your money to work for you. Now you can create an action plan by defining the precise steps that will help you achieve your dreams. Each of those steps will be a goal, and your action plan will help you hit your deadlines for those goals.

Purse story: Planning to succeed

From the time she was a teenager, Tamika Smith dreamed of being the next Connie Chung. Tamika admired Chung, the Emmy-award-winning television journalist and daughter of immigrants who broke barriers by becoming the first person of Asian descent to anchor the national news on network television, and the first female co-anchor of *CBS Evening News*. Tamika was the daughter of Bahamian–Haitian immigrants, and she wanted to follow in Connie Chung's footsteps but also break new ground. She believed education would pave the way for the future she dreamed of, including providing her with financial success and security.

On her journey to achieve her goals, Tamika attended Howard University, in Washington, DC, and was excited to land an internship with National Public Radio after graduation. Shortly after that, she got her first job as a news anchor with *The Al Sharpton Show*, where she earned an annual salary of $30,000. She was thrilled to be earning money in her chosen field and felt confident about paying back her student loans.

In 2008, six months after graduation, Tamika was hit with a double-whammy setback. She received a huge bill for her student loans at the same time that the nation's economy took a dramatic downturn. Tamika quickly realized she'd have trouble meeting her financial obligations with her current salary. "When I reached out to that specific loan company to share my hardship," she said, "that's when reality set in that I had to pay back that bill, no matter what."

Understand your value

A big part of Tamika's self-worth was tied up in the idea of paying back her debt, and she struggled to reconcile the notion that she wouldn't be able to pay off the enormous bill on her desired timeline. Finally, she decided she would get it done, no matter what. To stay on track with her loan payments, she took on multiple jobs – as many as she could juggle – knowing the extra work would be temporary. "I had to cut the fray out, get focused on what I wanted to do, and understand that this process was not going to be forever," she said, "but it was going to be for right now so that I could see myself through to the other side."

Tamika adopted a mindset of viewing her jobs as clients, and turning her skill set into a business to provide value for those clients. She also shifted her mindset to one of abundance and service. As you saw with Wealth Secret #2 – find your superpower – getting wealthy is a function of your ability to use your gifts and talents to serve others. To do that, you must understand your value. When Tamika focused on service, she better understood the value she could provide and discovered gaps she could fill.

Things began to look precarious again in Tamika's financial life in 2020, when the university and newsroom where she worked both experienced personnel shake-ups. Tamika had applied unsuccessfully for promotions two or three times, but she didn't let that stop her from trying again, and she decided to go all out when an opening arose in 2020. This time she created an electronic press kit (EPK), which served as a portfolio to showcase what she'd been doing outside of the university, in radio, television, and online media, and demonstrated how she could bring those resources to the university. The EPK, often used to distribute promotional materials to the media, was a way for Tamika to give her resume a level of pizzazz no other candidate had.

Tamika also listened to TED Talks to study how to effectively present. In one talk, she learned about the two-minute power pose, also known as the Wonder Woman pose, with hands on hips and feet shoulder-width apart. She used the power pose and listened to Beyoncé's "Diva" to get in the right frame of mind before heading into every interview. Tamika didn't wind up getting the role she applied for, but she was so impressive that the team found a different role for her.

Some people might have quit their extra jobs at this point, but Tamika kept hers. She had about ten years of experience with contracts, so she knew the role she had in radio wouldn't conflict with what she was doing in TV or on podcasts. She held on to her other clients because they created more income to fuel her plan.

"The first thing I would say, when it comes to strategy, is don't worry about how much you're making at this specific point in time," Tamika said. "What you need is a process because the process will then multiply when you have more money. If you have no process, then that same chaos is going to get multiplied when you get more money."

Tamika understood a basic principle: Without a wealth mindset, including a solid plan, more money only creates more chaos. Early in the process, she chipped away at the debt, throwing an extra ten or twenty dollars onto a payment when she could, but she didn't see much movement. She then made a strategic decision that required tons of discipline. She designated the full income from one of her jobs to pay off her student loans. She opened a bank account and deposited her paychecks into it without any second-guessing.

While depositing the paychecks into this special account, Tamika continued to make her regular loan payments. Her strategy was to pay off the smallest loan first to get a quick win. Interest starts accruing again after the payment cycle so to avoid interest accruing on the low balance remaining, she simply paid the entire balance. The plan made all the difference for her.

While Tamika worked her plan to pay off debt, she also saved money. Instead of being content to sock it away in a savings account, she had the wisdom to know she should strategically allocate those funds, and the humility to know she needed help in learning how to do so. She reached out to me so she could learn even more about how to maximize her investments.

Find your focus

Tamika credited her success to the mindset work she did early on her journey. Without understanding her relationship with money, all her strategy would have fallen flat. "If you have roots where you're not necessarily understanding your emotional connection to money, then it doesn't matter how much you make. You're always going to be spending, whether it's five, ten, one hundred, or a thousand dollars," she said. "So really, it's about a combination between understanding your emotional connection to the money and then being able to create strategy from that space. If you don't understand what your own personal beliefs are [about] money, then no program is really going to work for you." This shift in mindset allowed Tamika to become laser-focused on her goals and follow her plan.

Tamika said, "The light bulb clicked for me. Hey, it's not about what I'm doing – it's about who I am and what I'm bringing to the table. And I can apply this to anything else. And that's what really kind of planted the seed for me to be able to attack the goal of paying off my student loans."

To achieve anything of significance in life, you need a strong, internal, emotional reason for doing so. Many people refer to this reason as your "why," the underlying motivation behind *why* you do what you do. This motivation must be compelling enough to keep you focused on your goal when distractions, like opportunities to spend your money elsewhere, arise. When you set financial goals, you can't just pick a number. You need to know what those goals represent for you. For example, does the ability to travel where and how you want appeal to you? Are you shooting for early retirement, leaving a legacy for your children and grandchildren, or both?

For Tamika, becoming debt-free represented freedom. The appeal of freedom and a weight being lifted were far more powerful than just paying bills and watching her loan balances decrease. She wanted the *feeling* of freedom. She also took pride in paying her debts, and she harnessed that pride in a productive way to build her financial future.

The following exercises will help you clarify your goals and create a financial plan to make them a reality.

EXERCISE: CREATE A GOAL-FOCUSED ACTION PLAN

You've already identified what you need to feel fulfilled in your life. You likely have goals that include some combination of relationships, financial and physical security, spiritual connection, good health, travel and exploration, financial legacy, and intellectual satisfaction.

With that list of goals in front of you:

- Write down your compelling reason for each of the goals you desire.

- Put a monetary value to the goals that have a financial component. Don't guess at these costs – do the necessary research to clarify how much money you'll need to achieve each of the goals. For instance, if you want to move into a larger home in a specific neighborhood, look at the cost of those homes and the trend in home prices in that area.

- Outline the next steps you need to take. Perhaps you need to attend a seminar or get more financial education. Maybe you need to diversify your portfolio or open new accounts, or you need to reach out to a professional to help you in a specific area.

- Prioritize your list, according to which goal you want to accomplish first, second, and so on. Be sure to note your expected completion date beside your goals.

Remember: A goal is a dream with a timeline. You've identified what your dream is and why it's important to you. Having a goal-focused action plan is the key to flourishing and succeeding, despite the financial obstacles in your path. A timeline will make it much more likely that you'll execute on your plan and make your dreams a reality.

Tamika knew exactly how much money she needed to pay off each of her debts, and she had a strong motivation to do so. She prioritized the order in which she'd pay them off, and she laid out a timeline for payment. This is a great example of combining dreams with an action plan to create achievable goals.

Even as her situation changed, Tamika stayed focused. When she got a promotion, she could have dropped her extra jobs and relaxed, but she kept working her plan. She knew the job juggling would be temporary and would help her reach her goal by her desired deadline, as long as she followed through on the steps she'd laid out. The extra work allowed her to pay off her debts and give herself choices much sooner, all while also working toward her goal of building wealth in her investment accounts.

What financial dreams can you emotionally connect to? You'll encounter a lot of choices along the way, and your decisions will usually be a result of how badly you want those future rewards. Don't hesitate to dangle smaller rewards for yourself at each step. Use whatever tactics you need to keep moving and growing.

Put each dollar where it belongs

In early 2020, Tamika still had $40,000 of student loans, and her goal was to pay off those loans by December 31 of that year. With her plan in place, she knew she could do it. She stuck to her strategy and made the rounds at the banks, paying her loans, and by New Year's Day 2021, she was debt-free.

"January 1, 2021, I felt free for the first time in my life," Tamika said. "It was like a load had just melted off me, and all of the heartache, and the five or six jobs, and

strategizing, and doing all the things I needed to do...
I felt like, wow – everything I did, all the sacrifice I
made, was worth it."

Tamika was only able to achieve that goal because
she knew exactly what she owed and what she was
bringing in. She focused on those figures and created
a savings or investing account for each goal, based on
her timeline. Her plan included allocating income to
different accounts, including one to pay off her car loan,
another for student loans, and another for investments.
She kept following the process, and with the promotion
and an increase in pay, she was able to accelerate her
plan. She paid off the remainder of her debt within two
years and achieved a six-figure retirement portfolio at
the same time.

Treat your financial planning and investments like
a business. Review your statements regularly. Keep
track of your bills and maintain accurate records for
your investments and other accounts, such as your
savings accounts for short-term goals. Continue to use
your superpower to add value and come up with an
initial deposit for any investments you need to make to
achieve your goals. It doesn't matter whether you have
a little or a lot to work with right now. The important
thing is to develop a habit of working your plan; then,
as you bring in more income, you'll easily put that
money where it needs to go to reach your goals.

Sticking to the plan isn't always easy. Distractions,
temptations, and life events – positive or negative – will

arise and challenge you to find a way to keep going in the direction of your goals. However, your wealth mindset will keep you going in the face of adversity, even when people tell you your goals are impossible. Tamika had far more student debt than she could pay off with her dream job, but she also had self-motivation, and she created a plan. She figured out how to become debt-free even though she started her journey during a recession.

Above all, stay focused on the end game. Today you can get minute-by-minute updates on every account and investment, but that won't help you achieve your goals. In fact, it can distract you from your plan. Awareness does not mean obsessing or being reactive; it simply means you know your numbers. Revisit your goals once or twice a year and check whether they're still aligned with what you want to accomplish. If your plans have changed, you can always move in a new direction. Flexibility is key.

As you set goals and take action to achieve them, you'll need the right team around you. This includes professionals whose expertise and insight you trust. Although you are responsible for your financial future, the input from these team members will be invaluable as you make decisions. Your team may include a tax professional, a financial planner, an attorney to help you protect your assets, a wealth coach to review your progress and help you stay accountable for your goals, and an estate-planning attorney. We'll get into some of this in more detail, but for now, know that you want to surround yourself with experts you trust. No one builds wealth alone.

Goal-driven spending and decision making

On her journey to wealth, Tamika committed to understanding her relationship with money. She looked at how she typically spent money and shifted her mindset to view money as a tool rather than a means to gratification. Unnecessary spending might feel good in the moment, but Tamika recognized she would also end up feeling guilty. She focused on her plan but didn't beat herself up when she failed to follow the plan exactly. "Give yourself grace," she suggested.

As Tamika discovered, when you have a goal that's clearly rooted in your values and you have an action plan, it's easier to make sound money decisions. You don't get distracted by the latest shiny objects, and you're better able to determine what will keep you on track and what could send you on a detour. With an income mindset, cash on hand drives your purchasing decisions, but when you have a wealth mindset, your goals drive your spending. You focus on making sure your inflow exceeds your outflow so you have money to invest. You seriously consider whether any significant purchase will help you grow wealth.

It's amazing how quickly you can switch your thinking to look at a potential purchase and imagine how much stock you could buy for its price tag. Redirecting your resources makes a big difference, because it allows you to put the power of growth and compounding to work through your investments. Eventually, you'll discover how gratifying it feels to buy something without guilt because you know you've been smart with your money. With a solid action plan, your spending is always intentional and aligned with your plan.

Mindset: Retirement planning

Tamika had been saving for some years when she decided to focus on getting her retirement portfolio to six figures. When she worked for a large tech company, she took advantage of the employer match for her 401(k), even though she was only just starting to learn about investments. Tamika knew that wouldn't be enough to achieve her retirement goals, though, so she also invested in a Roth IRA. These accounts allowed her to keep her retirement investments separate from the money dedicated to paying off her student loans and other debts. "It's funny," Tamika said of the moment she realized she had six figures in her retirement accounts. "When you hit [that number], you don't even realize you do because everything is so separate. You sit down and pull out the trusty notepad, and it's like – wait a minute – I just hit six figures!"

When you think about your goals, be sure to include retirement. You're never too young or too old to make a goal-focused action plan for the time when you're no longer working. The plan will look different depending on your age now, the age you plan to retire, and your vision of retirement. Have you thought about what you'll need in your retirement? Consider your must-haves as well as your wildest desires. Remember to think about what those dreams stand for and what they feel like. Is it peace of mind? Independence? Security?

It's important to get specific when envisioning your retirement, just as you would any other goal. Many people say they want to retire comfortably, but what does that mean? Will you live in your own home, and will it be the same place you're in now? Will you travel, and if so, how often? Do you know your future budget for living expenses, healthcare, and hobbies? Write those numbers down and create your wealthy-lifestyle retirement plan.

Some people resist retirement planning because they don't want to think about growing old. This too is a matter of mindset. Women focused on building wealth understand they don't have time for avoidance. They take action now, and they prioritize their needs. They recognize they can take care of themselves financially, and they know it's unrealistic to expect someone else to swoop in and handle things.

EXERCISE: HOW TO SHIFT YOUR THINKING IF YOU HAVEN'T PLANNED FOR RETIREMENT

The same as with any of your other financial goals: Consider your deadline, how much money you'll need by then, and the steps to take to get there. Prioritize what comes first and what comes next.

Make a list of all your retirement goals, the monthly expenses of those goals, and the source of income for those expenses:

Retirement goal	Monthly expense	Source

Now that you have your plan, commit to it, but be flexible. Understand that life happens, and be prepared to pivot your plan when necessary.

If you're feeling just a little intimidated about (or completely overwhelmed by) the idea of figuring out where to put the money for your different goals, that's perfectly reasonable. There's always an element of risk to investing, but in the next chapter, you'll learn the fundamentals of managing your investments to balance risk and reward.

7
Wealth Secret #5: Recognize Problems As Opportunities

Investing to get wealthy requires a long-term focus. You can learn all the Wealth Secrets, but you also have to prepare yourself for the fact that world and market events will, at times, test your resolve. This is when the importance of diversification becomes impossible to ignore and the wealthy look for opportunities to take advantage of problems in the market.

There's no better contemporary example of this than the economic uncertainty created by the COVID-19 pandemic and the subsequent volatility in the stock market. As stock prices fell, many investors pulled money from places they thought were too risky and looked for safer bets. The impact and response were similar to the reaction folks had during the 2008 recession, but not nearly as bad as when the stock market crashed on October 19, 1987 – a day that came to be known as Black Monday. I had just started as a receptionist at Merrill Lynch, and I saw panic in the eyes of white-collar and blue-collar workers from the auto industry. Prior to that day, I would greet them as they came into the lobby, during their lunch breaks, to watch our electronic stock sticker; or I would take phone calls asking for the latest quote on General Motors, Ford, or Chrysler. Many clients of the firm had put all their savings in their employers' stock and had limited knowledge of investing and how to build a portfolio. As a result of this lack of knowledge, they panicked and moved their money to less risky vehicles such as bonds. It may have felt like a good move at the time, but in many cases, being overly conservative and reactive cost those clients thousands of dollars as the market recovered.

Although we often think of risk in terms of being overly aggressive or careless – behaviors we've most recently seen with cryptocurrencies and related fraud – we also take unnecessary risk when we're overly cautious. Just ask all the people who took their money out of stocks after the 2008 stock market crash and wound up missing the next bull market. Because they let fear dictate their actions, their losses compounded. With Wealth Secret #5 – recognize problems as opportunities – you'll position yourself to weather the ups and downs of the financial markets without panicking. You'll do this through diversification and by leveraging stock market volatility like the wealthy do.

Purse story: Playing the long game

Sophonia Hardaway first learned about diversification at a young age by observing her parents and grand-parents, who earned income from a variety of sources. Her father worked as a barber and a steelworker; and her grandfather worked a manufacturing job, with a side hustle as a grave digger. "I always saw multiple things going on in the family," Sophonia said. "And then they slowly went into real estate, and they started buying houses."

As she grew up, Sophonia took on the belief that she could also create multiple sources of income. She often had roommates, and she thought of the rent they paid her as "extra money." She might not have realized it at the time, but Sophonia was laying the foundation for her future wealth. Having multiple income sources provides a safety net in case one source disappears because of a job loss, a disaster, or a dip in one of the markets.

There's a difference between minimizing risk and play-ing it too safe. A savings account is low risk, but the interest rate will never keep up with the rate of inflation, so the reward is too low for it to be a wealth-building vehicle. The stock market, on the other hand, offers greater opportunity to make money, but the risk of losing money is also greater. No one wants to see their net worth headed in the wrong direction. However, the wealthy know downturns in the stock market can also provide opportunities to purchase assets at lower prices. I observed this on Black Monday, when the stock market fell by more than 20% in one day. Our wealthy clients came in later in the evening and met with their stockbrokers, and instead of selling, they added stocks from several blue-chip companies to their portfolios.

That was when I discovered Wealth Secret #5: Recognize problems as opportunities. Or, as the prolific investor Warren Buffett advises, "Be greedy when others are fearful." To reduce risk as an investor, continue to learn about the financial markets, and invest in a variety of investment products. Take action to make good decisions and to protect your money, but keep one thing in mind: As you've probably figured out by now, the truth is *there is no risk-free investment*. There's risk everywhere, whether you're parking money in a savings account or investing in stocks. The higher the potential risk, however, the higher the potential reward. That's why wealthy women take their time when choosing investments, and it's why diversification plays a major role in growing and protecting your wealth.

Diversification can lower your level of risk *and* increase your profits at the same time. Spreading your investments across a range of sectors reduces volatility in your portfolio. This way, if any particular category takes a sudden downturn, your other investments remain unscathed. When you consistently evaluate where you've focused your investments, and tweak accordingly, diversification protects your bottom line. While figuring all this out can seem intimidating, remember that the greatest risk is to take no risk at all. Being overly cautious stops you from finding opportunities in times of trouble and stunts your ability to get wealthy. The new financial normal requires you to embrace risk, change, and discomfort.

Build your investing confidence

Sophonia's parents wanted her to have opportunities they didn't, so they encouraged her to pursue higher education. Her father paid for her undergraduate education with cash, from which Sophonia learned that it's not how much money you make but what you do with it that determines your success. She decided she wanted to leave a legacy for her child too. Building on what her parents had taught her, she believed she could even do a little better than her parents had done because she earned more in her job as a systems engineer.

As is the case for almost everyone, Sophonia's formal education hadn't taught her much about money or building wealth. However, her schooling did teach her critical thinking skills, and it opened up opportunities for higher-paying jobs and an income she could leverage. It wasn't any school but rather her parents and grandparents who had planted the seeds of how she would develop wealth.

Sophonia always knew she wanted to diversify. It simply made sense to her based on what she'd seen her parents do, and she took a "slow walk," patient approach. For instance, she didn't rush into buying real estate as an investment, but when she moved into a larger house, she kept her townhouse and rented it out as an investment property. She bought insurance products to cover different scenarios and make sure she could take care of herself, no matter what happened. She also consistently contributed to her retirement accounts.

Keep evolving

Decades later, Sophonia started thinking about retiring early and was happy to discover the cash value of her insurance had added up. She used that money to buy into a franchise and left her retirement money to grow. Then, as a self-employed person, Sophonia sought out tax advantages available to business owners, and she reinvested her profits.

Despite her successes and thoughtful approach, Sophonia believed she should be even further along. She had always relied on financial advisors to make her investment decisions, but she'd come to realize the options they chose for her were a little too vanilla and too all-purpose. She was also bothered by the fact that most of the advisors she'd worked with couldn't adequately explain how any of their decisions affected her money. She searched for more information, and she eventually discovered WealthyU – a place where she could learn about investing so she could make more informed decisions.

"Putting all of your assets and all of your money that you work hard for into someone else's hands, it's not a good thing," Sophonia said. "We shouldn't do that. We should have some say in where we want our money to go, and we should have some say in how we want to invest it. I may not get it right all the time. But as long as I get within a percentage of what I'm looking for, for that year, I'm okay with that."

In WealthyU, Sophonia learned to research investments more deeply and to ask more questions. She also learned when to pivot and update her choices. When we talked not long after the height of the COVID-19 pandemic, Sophonia was going through all her assets and checking how diversified they were. This was part of her process of analyzing whether she was where she wanted to be and reaching the annual goals she had set. "Because the market is going up and down, I'm pretty safe," she said. "I think I did like 30% overall."

Like most people, Sophonia can sometimes get overwhelmed by all the information available, so she tries to take things at her own pace and continues her mantra of the slow walk. As she's gained confidence in her abilities, she's not only felt better about her finances, but she has also found her advisor respects her more and checks in with her more often. Where she might have gotten single-digit returns before, now she can get more of the stock index averages of double digits. "Yeah, it's a little bit, but it does add up over time with the compounding of the assets," she said. "So just the confidence itself, just knowing where you are financially, has been awesome for me."

Sophonia adopted all the Wealthy Secrets outlined here and taught in WealthyU. This included increasing her financial acumen so she could have better conversations with her financial advisor, more accurately assess her situation, and hold her financial advisor accountable. Her financial education allowed her to accelerate her financial growth. Then Sophonia was able to optimize and finally maximize her income by analyzing her investments for herself and in her business. She went back to her early role models of diversification and put those principles to work for her by developing a balanced portfolio and making changes to that balance when it made sense to do so.

Balance risk and reward

Prudent redistribution – as opposed to knee-jerk reactions – is a smart way to maximize your profits. This means you can't just "set it and forget it" when it comes to your investments. While you don't want to make reactive decisions based on short-term changes in the markets, you do want to stay aware of those changes. Just as importantly, you'll factor in any changes in your goals, timelines, and risk tolerance, and adjust your portfolio as needed.

One straightforward way to balance risk and reward is to consider your mix of stocks and bonds. Stocks are generally more subject to ups and downs, and bonds are typically more steady state. Stocks also typically provide a bigger return and higher profits, while bonds – with a set interest rate and maturity date – grow more slowly and consistently. Your portfolio should include the right mix of both, with a ratio tailored to your situation. This is referred to as asset allocation and should also include the amount of money you keep in cash, or in a savings or money market account, for short-term goals or emergencies.

In WealthyU, my wealth-coaching clients use my Asset Allocator to assess several factors and decide on their investment mix, based on their:

- Goals

- Knowledge of the market

- Age

- Risk tolerance

- Time frame for investing

We also talk about the average rate of return for various combinations and what their best twelve months and worst twelve months might look like, as well as their best and worst five years. This kind of analysis helps with long-range planning and thinking, so you're less likely to be enticed or scared into making rash decisions based on what the market is doing for any short period of time. To download a copy of the Asset Allocator, visit www.WealthyU.com/wealthsecrets.

While no one can tell you exactly what your investment mix should be, there are four rules of thumb you can use to make those decisions:

1. **If you're more than ten years away from your goal:** Bonds should make up less than 10% of your portfolio. You've got time to ride out ups and downs in the market, and you're looking at growth and the highest returns possible.

2. **If you're six to nine years from your goal:** Allocate about 30% of your portfolio to bonds. This offers a balance of growth and stability.

3. **If you're three to six years from your goal:** Consider investing more than 50% of your investment in bonds. In this way, when you need to access your money, you know your principal will be available. This is a good option for people who are saving for a down payment on a house, for example.

4. **If you're retiring soon:** You probably want more of your investments in defensive assets that

create income, like stocks that pay dividends and bonds that pay interest, so you can generate an income stream. Dividend stocks and bonds provide consistency; they are what wealthy people use as a defensive strategy during uncertain economic times and to take advantage of stock market volatility.

Using defensive investment strategies – conservative portfolio strategies designed to minimize the risk of losing the principal – can help you develop a wealthy focus. The slow and steady nature of these strategies gives you the peace of mind to handle the bigger fluctuations of the stock market. When you have a wealthy focus, you resist the temptation to follow the crowd, and you learn how to turn problems into opportunities. A wealthy focus helps you set priorities and eliminate distractions as you pursue your goals.

When diversifying, keep your personal tolerance for risk in mind. Are you seeking the potential for the greatest return and willing to take more risk? Or would you prefer a lower degree of risk, or some combination of the two?

Imagine what things would look like if the stock market dropped 20% and your investments dropped along with it. What would you do? Wealthy people see market downturns as an opportunity to buy more stock. At the other end of the spectrum, the average investor liquidates and transfers their investments into a money market account or some other low-risk, low-return vehicle. Other options include leaving your investments alone or selling some and leaving the rest where it is. Another strategy is dollar-cost averaging, where you invest systematically each month and buy shares at different prices. In this way, your average cost per share is typically reduced. Where you fall on this spectrum can help you understand your risk tolerance.

As you look to diversify your portfolio, keep your personal interests in mind. Invest in companies and products you understand or can learn about. Consider the tech boom at the turn of the millennium, when so many people got caught up in tech stocks and bought into the craze, even though they had no idea what they were purchasing. They lost a lot of money when that bubble burst. It's okay to take a chance on a hot investment, but diversification means you avoid putting all your money in one sector. You'll be taking an educated risk, not an emotional one.

Your personal life and your work life provide a range of ideas for investing. If you're a pharmacist, for example, you might look at pharmaceutical companies, but don't stop there. Expand your research to include related industries like medical technology or supplies, research companies, and more. Think about the car you drive, the clothes you wear, your hobbies, and your interests. You might want to factor into your investment research environmental or social justice issues that are important to you. Companies that work to create the change you desire to see in the world may be worth your consideration when you're deciding where to invest your money. Read about the companies behind the products you use and like, and if they're public, research how their stocks have performed before investing.

More ways to diversify

Your asset allocation goes beyond the *ratio* of stocks to bonds in your portfolio to include the *types* of stocks and bonds and funds, their sectors, and more. You diversify by investing money in a variety of vehicles, industries, and even nations. Putting some money into savings accounts (for short-term goals and emergencies) and retirement accounts is included in this process.

Let's say you've decided on a mix of stocks and bonds. Starting with stocks: What will they include? You can begin by identifying the sectors you're interested in and spread your risk among them. In addition to individual stocks, you can research mutual funds that concentrate on specific market sectors. (Mutual funds are where a group of investors pool their money to purchase a portfolio of investments run by a fund manager, and you share in the profits or losses of the fund as a whole.) As you look at your mix, you'll also consider small-cap, medium-cap, and large-cap funds (defined by the total number of shares multiplied by the share price).

As you diversify, you'll consider a mix of small-, medium-, and large-cap companies within your chosen sectors. Large-cap companies include Apple, Amazon, and Microsoft. Many mid-cap companies operate in specialized industries so are less likely to be household names, although you'll know names such as Dunkin', Skechers, and Texas Roadhouse. Finally, small caps are often young companies whose potential for growth is larger but whose risk is higher.

As you evaluate your choices, make sure you don't fall so in love with any one company or fund that you stake too much of your investment in it. Consider what would have happened if you'd had all or most of your investments in real estate in 2007, or everything tied up in the tech sector in 1999. Most advisors will recommend that a portfolio should not include more than 10% of any investment, including your employer's stock. You might be tempted to load up on your company's stock, but resist that temptation – if your company runs into financial trouble, you could lose your job and your investments in one fell swoop.

This work is important because, as I've noted, with proper asset allocation – based on your unique circumstances – you'll find it much easier to manage the ups and downs of the financial markets. No matter how hard you study and how much you learn, some losses are inevitable. Sometimes stocks or bonds simply don't perform the way your research led you to expect they would, or world events beyond your control affect the market in ways you couldn't possibly have predicted. Learn to absorb some loss and take the lessons. If you did your due diligence and things didn't work out in your favor, keep your cool and shrug it off. Wealthy women know that some loss is going to happen, and they take precautions to make sure those losses don't derail their entire plan.

The market fluctuates, but its success over time supports investing. Balancing risk and reward with smart asset allocation will make it easier for you to stay the course through all the market shakeups. Looking for opportunities where others see problems will allow you to increase your chances of coming out ahead. With Wealth Secret #6, in the next chapter, you'll learn how to leverage technology and put systems in place to research investments, get started investing, reduce the fees you pay, further minimize your risks, and automate where it makes sense to do so.

8
Wealth Secret #6: Leverage Tech And Systems

Now you understand the importance of diversifying your portfolio by balancing risk and reward, you might feel a little overwhelmed about the idea of managing and keeping track of it all. Just the process of researching your many options for stocks to invest in can seem like a huge task. How can you get comfortable taking educated risks with the money you generate as you increase your net worth and work to turn your income into wealth? You can leverage modern technology to make investing easier when you implement Wealth Secret #6: Leverage tech and systems.

Years ago, if you wanted to research investments, you had to go to the library. There you'd find the print versions of *Value Line* or *Morningstar* and drag them to a table, where you'd flip through the pages and take notes. Unless you could afford to work with a professional, it would have been difficult to know whether you correctly understood what you were looking at. Even worse, you needed thousands of dollars just to get started in the investing game. Brokerage firms could be – perhaps intentionally – intimidating to beginners, and sometimes even to an experienced investor. It might well have been daunting to think about speaking with a financial advisor or calling to make a purchase or a trade. All of this kept many middle-class people locked out and stuck right where they were.

Today you have right at your fingertips all the information you need to start investing. All you have to do is take advantage of that information. You can research stocks on your laptop, smartphone, or tablet and find information in seconds. You can educate yourself in the privacy of your own home and go through some trial and error before moving on to a more formal and more educated conversation with an advisor. Those resources we previously had to travel to the library to access are now easily available online, and there are many more of them.

You can also invest at a fraction of the cost. Where you used to need a minimum of $2,500 to get started, you can now log in to an app and buy fractional shares for as little as $5. Think about that. In 1978, for example, you needed a minimum of $2,500 to get started. Adjusted for inflation, that would be about $12,000 in 2023. Imagine that barrier to entry. With some of the investing apps available today, you can start buying fractional shares of stock for about the price of a fancy cup of coffee. Those same apps make it easy for you to automate your investing and to track your progress. There has never been a better time to get wealthy.

Purse story: Getting tech savvy

WealthyU student Xina Eiland is a prime example of how you can take advantage of technology to invest successfully for the long-term future. Xina is the president and CEO of X+PR, where she is a leader in digital strategy and event planning and an authority on multicultural communication. She is also the host of the *Get Found Get Funded* podcast, which features companies led by entrepreneurs from populations often underrepresented in the startup space. This might all sound glamorous, but Xina came to entrepreneurship the hard way. When she took leave from her job to have surgery, she came back only to find she'd been laid off. Rather than look for another job right away, Xina used her skill set as an asset, representing an author who came to her looking for PR help, and building her business from there.

Throughout the COVID-19 pandemic and the subsequent economic downturn, Xina's business thrived. Having not only bounced back after her layoff, but also having successfully made it through the 2008 economic collapse and recession, Xina was no stranger to navigating unexpected challenges. She looked to her experiences as evidence that she could weather whatever the pandemic brought to the economy. Xina reminded herself she had made it through once before, and she could do it again. She also held on to the fact that many people become rich – or get richer – during downturns.

"People are getting worried [about] inflation [and] gas prices," she said, when she joined me on my podcast, *Get Wealthy!*, to share her experience. "And all I'm doing is [saying], 'You know what, just pull it together, you're gonna get through this.' These are times where you take advantage of what's going on."

Xina took a hard look at her budget and her expenses to respond appropriately to market forces, and she kept saving and investing. When an unexpected car repair popped up, Xina learned a hard lesson. Luxury cars, she discovered, come with premium-priced repairs, and she was thankful that she had taken a crucial step. She had automated a lot of her investing and saving, so she had funds on hand that made what could have been a crisis easily manageable.

Capitalize on apps

I coach my clients in WealthyU to fit investing into their busy lives by systematizing it. One of the best ways to build wealth is to set up fail-safe ways to pay yourself first. When you set up systematic savings and investments, it becomes much easier to develop the discipline, focus, and habits to not only survive the ups and downs of the economy, but also to gain an advantage through dollar cost averaging. This process of investing the same amount at intervals allows you to purchase at different prices and prevents you from trying to time the market. Automating your savings and investing can help you recession-proof your finances so you thrive despite any periods of economic uncertainty.

You can use services through the payroll department at your job, through your bank, or through an investing app to automatically fund your savings accounts and, of course, to automatically invest in your retirement account. Tamika, who you met in Chapter 6, was masterful at setting up processes. She pointed out that how you behave when you have a little money is what you'll do when you have more, so be smart about it. Your process will get multiplied, for better or for worse. Start where you are, and increase the amounts you can save and invest over time.

Like Tamika, Xina figured out how to create systems that worked for her. Early on, she contributed to a 401(k) through her employer. Later, she was able to take dormant investment accounts and optimize them, and she started a new 401(k) through a relationship with a client.

Xina focused on diversifying. She invested in mutual funds and stocks, and then started investing in real estate. She relied on a couple of apps, which allowed her to automate budgeting and saving, to build her cash reserves. Digit allows users to budget for spending, bills, savings, and investing, and after an initial setup, the app will automatically transfer funds where the user directs them. (Digit has since rebranded as Oportun.) In 2022 Forbes Advisors ranked it one of the best budgeting apps.[14] Albert, a similar app, links to your checking and savings accounts and helps you track your finances, net worth, investments, and the like. Xina used the two different apps, setting one up for personal use and one for business purposes.

You can find a number of apps to help you actively budget, save, and track your spending. Every year, more and more apps are available to help you invest – this is an ever-evolving landscape. Because technology is always changing, make sure you research the latest information on any apps you're considering. If you're putting your money somewhere, make sure

---

14. B Holzhauer, "Digit Budgeting App Review" (Forbes Advisor, September 2, 2022), www.forbes.com/advisor/banking/digit -budgeting-app-review, accessed April 7, 2023

the company's accounts are properly insured so your money is protected if the app goes belly up.

An investing app such as Stash is a great way to learn the ropes and start building your portfolio. This is the technology that lets you start investing with small amounts of money. Once you reach about $10,000 invested, however, you'll want to open a brokerage account. When you choose an app to use for saving and investing, look at the maximum dollar amount the company insures (keeping in mind that you're not insured against potential losses in the market). Never accumulate more money with any one bank, investment company, or app than they can insure.

Some other apps for beginner investors include Acorns, Betterment, Public, Ellevest, and Robinhood. (Robinhood, though well known, is geared more toward day traders, ie, traders who buy and sell stocks within a single day, hoping to make a profit on short-term activity.) As with Stash, these apps allow you to invest for as little as $5 and purchase fractional shares – a great way to learn about the stock market before you start investing larger sums.

Regardless of which app you decide to use, most have similar features: search, research, learning, and investment capabilities. With an app like Stash, everything occurs online; there's no brick-and-mortar location to visit. They're partnered with a bank, but you can't walk in and speak with a teller. You can call customer service or message them with questions, so you might consider communication channels and responsiveness when you make your choice.

Stash doesn't charge transaction fees when you buy and sell stock, but you will pay a wrap fee – a monthly subscription fee to cover account management and administration costs. At the time of writing, Stash subscriptions ranged from $3 a month to $9. At the higher amount, you can even open custodial accounts for minors, whether that's your children, your grand-children, or even your neighbor's kids. A custodial account is a great way to teach kids about investing and get them interested, educated, and creating wealth from a young age.

With Stash you can open a personal portfolio and/or an individual retirement account (IRA), and you can also peruse products like life insurance. In addition, Stash offers Stock-Back® Rewards associated with their debit card. You'll earn pennies at a time in stock, but that's money you wouldn't otherwise have, which can add up every time you shop at Walmart or buy a coffee at Starbucks.

Utilize automation

One of the most important features of apps like Stash is automation. You can set up regularly scheduled automatic withdrawals from your bank to invest in a specific stock, an ETF, or a general portfolio fund, from which you later decide where to distribute the money. I suggest you see the whole process through and decide in advance where that money will be invested each time you make a transfer. When you regularly invest a fixed amount, over time, investing becomes a habit for you. You also eliminate the risk of forgetting the money is waiting for you to decide where it should go.

I can't stress enough how important it is to automate your investments. It's too easy to spend the money elsewhere if you have it sitting in your checking account, not to mention how often we simply forget to move funds. I once discovered I'd contributed a bunch of money to a SEP (simplified employee pension) plan, and left it in the money market fund without investing the money in stocks or stock mutual funds, but automated systems ensure it happens less. Don't trust yourself to remember.

These apps also offer varying levels of research capabilities, which can provide you at least with basic information on stocks you're considering, information – dividends, position, current trading – and market news. A brokerage account will offer you more research options than an app, and it's another place to diversify once you're ready. In a brokerage account, you can trade stocks, bonds, ETFs, and mutual funds. You can do a lot online, just like with an app, but you can also open a brokerage account with a company that has a physical location, where you can go in and meet with someone face to face. You can open as many brokerage accounts as you like and invest as much money as you want or are able to. You have the option to manage your own accounts or choose a managed brokerage account.

When you're ready to access a more expanded array of products and services, typically after you have reached $10,000 in market value, you'll need a full-service brokerage account. This type of account will allow you to set up a stock watchlist where you can keep an eye on the price movements and performance of companies that you may decide to add to your portfolio in the future. Organizations that provide brokerage accounts include Fidelity Investments, TD Ameritrade, Charles Schwab, and Merrill.

Evaluate mutual funds

When Xina started working with me, I discovered her investments were spread out over multiple mutual funds, and some were getting better returns than others. I walked her through a process to evaluate each of her mutual funds and compare their performance. With that information, she was able to consolidate those investments into just a few of the better-performing mutual funds. Just as with stocks, we have a methodical way to evaluate mutual funds.

In WealthyU, our members learn how to do this research on their own. However, they also have the opportunity to complete worksheets that walk them through these steps, compare notes, and ask questions of each other and our group experts. We go in depth together, so our clients can feel confident in their research. We walk them through exactly how to read the charts they find online and how to interpret the data they find.

Create a stock watchlist

During the early part of the COVID-19 pandemic, Xina decided to cut back on spending. It wasn't difficult, since trips and outside-the-home entertainment were out, but Xina took it a step further. Rather than order all her meals from DoorDash, as many people started doing, Xina said, "I started learning how to cook better and cooked more." She also looked at her subscriptions and found an extra $300 she could trim from her monthly expenses. She put those savings to good use. "There are some [stocks] that have come down that I wanted to buy before but they were just a little bit too high. Now, they're at a point where I can buy [them]. So I've been buying more stock." Because she had been watching those stocks, she saw an opportunity and was able to take advantage of it.

As you get more serious about investing, you'll need a way to keep track of the various stocks that catch your interest. An investment might sound interesting when you first hear about it, but that doesn't mean you jump right in and buy. You might decide to watch it for a while to see how it's trending, or you might have your eye on a stock whose price is currently too high. In that case, you want to set a buy price for it and keep tabs on it.

You need an organized way to keep track because you can't keep information on dozens of stocks in your head. I recommend setting up a stock watchlist, which is exactly what it sounds like.

Here are the steps to set up a watchlist through Yahoo Finance:

1. Head to Yahoo.com and click "Sign In" at the top of the page.

2. After logging in (or creating an account if necessary), click "Finance" at the top of the page.

3. Choose "My Portfolio" and then "Create a Portfolio." Give it a name and click "Submit."

4. Click the "Add Symbol" button and type in the name or symbol of the stock you want to watch.

5. Click on "My Holdings." This will open a chart with columns, which allows you to choose information that shows you what happens with the stock over time.

6. Enter the date, enter 1 share, and type in the stock price for the date, which you'll be able to see in the Market Value column. You can also add notes here.

That's it, and from here, you can customize even more. You'll automatically start out with the "Fundamental" view, which provides basic information, but you can click "Create View" to mix things up. You might want to see your stocks' percentage change rather than dollar-value change, for example. You can find the price-to-earnings value, information on dividends, sales, cost per share, and more. You can also play around with the dates to see historical data.

Yahoo Finance is just one place where you can set up a watchlist. Do your research and choose the site that works best for you.

Do your research

You wouldn't spend money in your business without having a plan and knowing your money would be put to good use, so why treat your personal accounts any differently? It all starts with good research. You can find any number of websites, news outlets, and podcasts touting financial advice and access to research. Once you know what you're looking for, it's simply a matter of choosing the resources you trust the most and find the easiest to use.

Keep in mind that technology changes fast, so check for the latest information. I recommend starting with the tried and true Morningstar, which has been around since 1984 and is one of the leading websites for investment research. You can use a number of tools on the site to research stocks, bonds, ETFs, and mutual funds; create watchlists; and track your portfolio across accounts. You can also get personalized tips and insights based on your portfolio.

General information on some valuable sources at the time of writing:

- Yahoo Finance provides stock quotes, financial news, personal finance tools, and tools for research and analysis. You can also keep tabs on your portfolio using this site.

- TipRanks is an AI-powered research technology company on a mission to simplify stock research. It aggregates information from thousands of analysts and news sources. You can find buy, hold, and sell ratings plus price targets from experts and also see those analysts' success ratings, among other research tools.

- Most of the investment apps, like Stash and Acorns, have some research capabilities. Remember these websites and apps are changing all the time – adding features and trying to do more to win your business – so evaluate several and decide which works best for you.

- Diving into resources like CNBC, The Motley Fool, NerdWallet, Google Finance, and *Barron's* can help you develop your knowledge, vocabulary, and comfort level around investing.

Research and analyze

One of the benefits enjoyed by members of WealthyU is the opportunity to discuss their research and learn together. Researching investments can be intimidating when you first start, but when you see other people doing it, you'll gain confidence that you can do the same. It's always helpful to have a community where you can ask questions about investments and get feedback. We have a treasure trove of resources, including teaching sessions, worksheets, and PDFs, and we continually host "Research and Analyze" sessions. In these coach-led sessions, members get to follow my exact process for making a decision about whether or not to buy a stock.

It can be tempting to rely on the experts to do the research for you, and it makes sense to get expert input. However, once you learn how to do this work for yourself, you'll develop a new level of confidence in your decision making. You'll undo any dependency you have on other people to choose when to buy, hold, or sell any particular stock. Most of all, you'll be empowered to go against the crowd, when past and present data support that choice, so you can find opportunities where other investors only see problems.

Simply and bluntly put: You don't have to be a rocket scientist to learn how to research investments. You just need some basics and some discipline, and you'll be well on your way. This book has given you enough to get off to a good start.

Creating wealth gets easier, and opportunities open up for you when you no longer have to rely solely on other people's advice to make investment decisions. As you become more knowledgeable, take more action, and amass more wealth, you'll need to take steps to preserve your assets. In the next chapter, you'll learn how to protect the wealth you're building, with Wealth Secret #7: Protect what you build.

9
Wealth Secret #7: Protect What You Build

If you're like most of my clients, your desire to get wealthy isn't all about you. Now that you've learned six of the Wealth Secrets, you can envision something bigger. You have loved ones you want to support in times of need. You have goals that will outlive you. You also want to be able to pay forward the most valuable asset of all: the knowledge of how to build wealth. Wealth Secret #7 – protect what you build – will show you how to accomplish all that.

Purse story: Essential safeguarding

My client, Belinda Edwards, went from being financially timid and feeling behind on retirement planning to building a growing legacy beyond what many people imagine they could have. As a young woman, early in her IT career, Belinda immersed herself in learning all she could about computers. What she didn't learn along the way was personal finance, how to invest, or how to preserve her wealth once she created it.

"My belief primarily was that a savings account was really good," said Belinda, "and that if I were to invest in the stock market, it should be in the most conservative fund because that was the safest fund." She focused more on not losing money than she did on making gains, and it showed in her results.

As the years passed, Belinda grew more aware of the reality of her financial situation. She realized that if she kept going the same way, she wouldn't be prepared for the kind of retirement she wanted. Belinda was also a self-described emotional spender, but after we met and she heard my story, she began to shift her mindset around money. She recognized she needed to do the work to develop a wealth mindset. "I was able to understand some of the triggers that I had related to money as well as how I could work on those triggers," said Belinda. She also learned my techniques to research stocks and mutual funds, and she made use of those tools.

"At one point," said Belinda, "I was working for Visa and MasterCard, not for myself." Retail therapy, she realized, wasn't her friend. In addition to desiring more financial freedom and the ability to achieve long-term goals for herself, Belinda wanted the financial where-withal to help her parents, should there be a need. These desires motivated her to keep learning and to keep making better choices.

"Having long-term goals, I had to change my mindset to know that savings really wasn't enough – that I needed to take a chance in the stock market," said Belinda. "And, more importantly, I needed to work with someone like yourself, who could help me understand what I didn't already know. [I learned] it was okay to take a risk because, as you said, there's no reward without taking some risk."

For the first time, Belinda developed an annual budget, which she assessed once a quarter. She created account-ability relationships to help her stay on track, and she began to pull all the investment opportunity levers at her disposal. She also took advantage of her employer's relationship with an investment company, meeting with her investment advisor on a monthly basis, and she purchased long-term care insurance. Belinda was beginning to think and act like a wealthy person. She had discovered our final Wealth Secret and was making moves to create a legacy. The wealthy trust themselves first, and they take the necessary steps to protect their assets and preserve them for future generations. This is exactly what Belinda did.

Tax-advantaged accounts

Having worked her way up to a six-figure income, Belinda wisely participated in her company's retirement savings plan and took advantage of the maximum employer contribution match. This allowed her to take full advantage of the tax benefits associated with the account. Tax-advantaged accounts offer tax benefits such as deferral of taxes, or tax exemptions. Tax-advantaged retirement savings plans include a 401(k), 403(b), 457, IRA, and/or Roth IRA. Each offers tax advantages for your retirement savings, as summarized here:

1. **401(k), 403(b), or 457:** A 401(k), 403(b), or 457 allows you to contribute pretax money up to annual limits set by the IRS. That means you don't pay taxes on that percentage of your salary. These accounts also allow you to defer the tax on the interest your investments earn. If your employer offers a match to your contribution, it's wise to contribute enough to max out that match. Otherwise, you're leaving money on the table.

2. **Roth IRA:** A Roth IRA is a little different from those other retirement accounts. For this account, you contribute *post-tax* dollars. You've already been taxed on the money you invest, but the gains you earn are exempt from taxes. At the time of writing, most investors can make tax-free

withdrawals from a Roth IRA after the age of fifty-nine and a half. You can also withdraw up to $10,000 from the account for a first-time home purchase at any age and without penalty.

3. **Traditional IRA:** A traditional IRA allows you to make contributions with your pretax or after-tax income. This is another instance when the tax is deferred on your money's growth. You can make withdrawals at age fifty-nine and a half, just as with a Roth IRA, but in this case, the withdrawals are taxed at your current income at the time of withdrawal.

4. **Retirement savings accounts:** Retirement savings accounts are the kinds of tax-advantaged accounts you're most likely to start with as you build your investment portfolio. Choosing the one or multiple accounts right for you will depend on your options with your employer, your income, your age, and your goals.

5. **529 college savings plan:** A 529 college savings plan allows the money you invest to cover current private school expenses and future higher education costs for a child – not necessarily your own child – to grow tax-free. This account has no income limitations, which means, regardless of how much you earn, you can still invest in a 529 account. You can also choose your risk level by choosing the mutual fund your money is invested in.

These funds can only be used for education costs, not for that spring break trip your child will one day want to take, so they're safely earmarked to cover tuition, fees, books, supplies, room and board, and other qualified expenses. Your investment grows tax-free, and as long as you use the money for what it was earmarked to cover, your withdrawals are also exempt from federal tax. (State taxes vary by state.) A recent tax law change now allows leftover funds in 529 plans of up to $35,000 to be rolled into a Roth IRA if the account has been established for at least five years.

The 529 prepaid tuition account is one of my favorite tax-advantaged accounts. Anyone can invest in this account for a minor, and you have the option of investing a lump sum or paying in monthly installments. Here's the beauty of this account: The cost of tuition is frozen at the time when you start making contributions. Once the state has determined the cost of tuition and fees will be a specified amount when the child goes to college, that number can never go up for you. These accounts enjoy the same tax benefits as a regular 529 plan.

Keep two things in mind with prepaid tuition accounts:

1. They tend to be tied to a specific state, and if your child decides to attend an out-of-state institution or a private university, the plan will

pay the national public-school average. You will be responsible for any difference. The higher-education opportunities available in your state will make a big difference in deciding if this is the right plan for your family.

2. These accounts only cover tuition costs. You'll need other investments and savings to cover the cost of room and board and other expenses.

Insurance

Few people would spend tens of thousands of dollars on a new car and fail to insure it, yet a 2022 study revealed that only 46% of women had a life insurance policy.[15] Many of those women are likely underinsured as well. Don't fall into that trap – sufficient life insurance should always be part of your wealth plan. You are your greatest asset.

When insurance comes up in conversation, people often think of a life insurance policy that pays a specified amount of money on the death of the insured person. Wealthy people know there are different types of insurance that insure against different types of risks.

---

15. M Backman, "Women Are Less Likely to Have Life Insurance Than Men. Here Are 3 Reasons They Aren't Buying It" (the ascent, a Motley Fool service, June 10, 2022), www.fool.com/the-ascent /insurance/life/articles/women-are-less-likely-to-have-life -insurance-than-men-here-are-3-reasons-they-arent-buying-it, accessed April 7, 2023

Life insurance

Life insurance is crucial for anyone on whose income their dependents or loved ones rely. In the event of your untimely death, life insurance can provide your loved ones with financial support to cover expenses such as funeral costs, outstanding debts, and living expenses. There are two main types of life insurance:

1. **Term life insurance:** Provides coverage for a specific period

2. **Permanent life insurance:** Provides coverage for your entire life

It's important to assess your needs and research the options before choosing the type of coverage that best fits your situation.

One of the key benefits of life insurance as an investment vehicle is the tax advantages it offers. Depending on the type of policy you choose, you may be able to build up cash value that grows tax-deferred within the policy. This means you won't owe taxes on the growth until you withdraw the funds, giving you more flexibility in how you manage your money.

While there are many benefits to using life insurance as an investment vehicle, it's important to also consider the potential downsides. One key factor to keep in mind is the cost of the policy. Life insurance can be more expensive than other investment options, especially if you are older or have health issues. Additionally, if you decide to cash out the policy early, you may face surrender charges or other fees that could eat into your returns.

Another potential downside of life insurance is that it can be more complex and difficult to understand than other investment products. There are many different types of policies available, each with its own set of features and benefits, and it can be challenging to navigate the options and choose the right one for your needs. Additionally, life insurance is often sold by commission-based agents, which means they may have an incentive to recommend more expensive policies or ones that aren't the best fit for you.

Finally, it's important to remember life insurance is just one tool in your financial toolbox. It shouldn't be the only investment you rely on for building wealth. While life insurance can provide valuable benefits and protection, it's important to also consider other options like stocks, bonds, real estate, or retirement accounts, to create a diversified portfolio that can help you reach your long-term goals.

Life insurance can be a powerful tool for creating a wealthy legacy, offering tax advantages, death benefits, and flexibility, all of which can help you meet your financial goals. However, it's important to carefully consider the potential costs and complexity of life insurance and to remember that it should be just one piece of your overall investment strategy.

Disability insurance

Disability insurance is designed to protect your income if you become unable to work due to an injury or illness. This type of insurance can provide you with a portion of your income while you are unable to work, helping you cover essential expenses such as rent, utilities, and food.

It's even more important for women to consider disability insurance because they are more likely to experience a disability than men due to factors such as pregnancy and childbirth. When choosing disability insurance, consider the waiting period, benefit period, and coverage amount to ensure that you have adequate protection.

Health insurance

Health insurance is essential for everyone, regardless of gender. However, as a woman, you may have unique health needs that require additional coverage. For example, you may need coverage for pregnancy and childbirth, mammograms, or other women's health services.

When choosing health insurance, consider the deductibles, copayments, and out-of-pocket maximums to ensure that you have affordable coverage that meets your needs.

Long-term care insurance

Long-term care insurance is designed to cover the costs associated with long-term care, such as nursing home care, assisted living, or in-home care. As women tend to live longer than men, they may be more likely to need long-term care in their later years. Long-term care insurance can help protect your assets and ensure that you receive quality care in the event that you need it.

As Belinda developed her wealth-building skills and saw her money growing, she thought more about how she would protect the legacy she was building. For the first time, she purchased long-term care insurance. Many of us dismiss this important insurance product, especially in our younger years, when we often feel invincible. These policies are designed to help with costs not covered by the typical health insurance, like assisted living or nursing home care.

Depending on where you live, assisted living can cost upwards of $4,000 a month. Nursing homes, which provide a higher level of care, can cost much more, ranging upwards of $7,000 a month for a semiprivate room. Imagine how quickly your wealth could be depleted if you had to pay for nursing home care, completely out of pocket, for a year, two years, or more. Long-term care insurance can cover some of that cost for you, allowing you to hold on to the assets you might otherwise have to liquidate. A qualified insurance professional can help you decide the right time to buy a policy and which policy is best for you.

Belinda felt grateful to be in a position to help her parents when they fell ill. "I was able to financially weather our storm and provide financial support to my parents. I was able to care for myself, where I didn't feel the [financial] pain," she said. "I wouldn't have been able to do that if I was still just saving."

As you build wealth, you can position yourself to do the same for your parents or other loved ones, should they ever need your support. However, depending on your parents' ages, you might also talk with them and guide them to consider sufficient life insurance, especially for a partner or spouse who might be left behind, and long-term care insurance. All insurance is designed to help you mitigate risk. If you have it and never truly need it, you're lucky. If you don't have it when you need it, you're in trouble.

Health savings account

A health savings account (HSA) is a component of a high-deductible health insurance plan that allows you to set aside money on a pre-tax basis. You can withdraw as needed for qualified medical expenses. When you deposit money into an HSA, you reduce your taxable income. When you withdraw those funds to use them for an eligible expense, that withdrawal isn't taxed.

Think about that: You don't pay tax on the contributions or the distributions. In addition, you don't pay taxes on the interest earned.

Some companies offer a flexible spending account (FSA) rather than an HSA. Those accounts are less flexible and have different tax consequences. For example, the money you contribute to an FSA is on a "use it or lose it" basis. If you don't use it for qualified medical expenses within the year, you forfeit those funds. An FSA and an HSA aren't the same, so pay attention to what you're signing up for.

If you're covered by an eligible high-deductible health insurance plan, consider how much money you might be wasting if you don't contribute to an HSA. Prescriptions, medical procedures, and co-pays all add up, especially if you or your dependents have an ongoing medical condition or a medical emergency now or in the future. Don't pay tax on the money you'll use for those expenses if you don't need to.

As of 2023, you could contribute up to $3,850 for an individual plan, or a maximum of $7,750 for a family plan. At age fifty-five or older, you're allowed to contribute an additional $1,000 on top of those figures. Any funds you don't use roll over and remain in your account. If you withdraw money for non-eligible expenses prior to age sixty-five, you'll pay a penalty plus federal income tax; after age sixty-five, you'll pay just the federal income tax. Learn more about HSAs and find the latest contribution limits at HealthCare.gov.

Estate planning

As with the insurance products above, too few people have a will in place when it's needed. When musical superstar Prince died unexpectedly, at just fifty-seven years old, he had no will indicating how he wanted his assets distributed. It took years for the court to sort out his estate, which was worth more than $150 million. His heirs most assuredly missed out on some of the estate-planning strategies that could have further preserved his legacy. At the other end of the spectrum, when iconic singer Aretha Franklin died, four different wills – three of them handwritten – turned up. The conflicting wills created confusion, delaying the distribution of her assets.

While those are the stories that make the news, celebrities aren't the only ones who deal with these problems. Countless times, I've met with a client and discovered they were dealing with probate issues and the headache that came with them. Someone in their family had died without a will or trust, and because there were several heirs, the proceeds from the estate were being litigated. This never has to happen to your heirs if you take the time for careful estate planning, including having a will drawn up.

Every adult who has children or any property or assets should have a will, which is simply a legal document that details how your property will be distributed to your heirs on your passing. It can also assert your other wishes, like who will be the guardian(s) for any minor children you have. Without a will, some of those decisions may end up being made by government agencies or a judge.

A will is a good start, but there are also other estate-planning documents you should have in place. In the event that you're rendered unconscious or incapacitated by illness or injury, a living will – also called an advanced healthcare directive – can specify your wishes for the medical care used to keep you alive. It allows you to dictate in advance whether and under what circumstances you'd want to be treated with CPR, palliative care, tube feeding, and other measures. You can also share your wishes for organ donation, or even donating your body, after your death.

A power of attorney allows you to appoint someone you trust to make financial and legal decisions for you. (You can also appoint a medical power of attorney.) In the event that you're unable to make decisions for yourself, perhaps due to an accident or an incapacitating illness such as dementia, the appointed person steps in to manage your affairs for you. When you think of the assets you're amassing and the wealth you're creating, you can see how important it is to have a power of attorney and to choose the right person for that responsibility. Belinda transformed from an overspender, afraid to invest in anything she deemed risky, to an investor in the top 10% of African–American wealth. You can do the same, but whatever gains you make in the meantime are worth protecting.

In addition to these documents, a trust can help you preserve the wealth you're creating. It allows you to transfer property to your chosen heirs – usually your loved ones – without the hassle of probate, which is the legal process by which a will is recognized and an executor is appointed for the estate. In some cases, a trust allows you to transfer property without subjecting the assets to gift taxes or estate taxes.

A qualified estate-planning attorney can help you decide which documents or vehicles you need and can draw up a will, living will, trust, and/or power of attorney for you. If you have aging parents, it's important to talk with them about their estate planning and any documents they've drawn up, especially if there's a chance you'll be responsible for some of their care in the event that their needs escalate.

It can be difficult to have these conversations with your parents, your spouse or partner, or your adult children. It can also feel stressful to make these decisions for yourself. After all, estate planning requires you to deal with the fact that you'll one day lose your parents, and your children or other loved ones will one day lose you.

However, these steps comprise one of the greatest gifts one generation can give to the next. You're working hard and investing your resources to grow your wealth, so do what wealthy people do: Protect what you build, and create a legacy.

At this point in your journey, you've learned the seven Wealth Secrets – the strategies I walk my clients through, step by step, in WealthyU. I hope you've started taking action on what you've learned. Remember: Knowledge is not power. Knowledge correctly applied is power. Get into community with like-minded women focused on similar goals. Start pulling together your team for support, accountability, and professional advice, and implement what you've learned here.

In the next chapter we'll go beyond the basics. You'll learn to finesse your finances with high-net-worth strategies most people will never know about, much less access. With these methods, you'll have the ability to join an elite class of the wealthy.

10
Bonus Wealth Secret: Employ High-Net-Worth Strategies

Before you dive into this chapter, I want to encourage you to stop and take a moment to acknowledge what you've accomplished so far. You've discovered the seven Wealth Secrets I share with the members of my private wealth-coaching community. Right now, you have more knowledge about how to get wealthy than most people will ever have. Let that sink in, and as you do, look forward to consistently applying this information now and for the rest of your life. Hopefully, you've already started taking action on what you've learned. If not, now is the time to get started. I'll say it again: Knowledge is not power. Knowledge correctly applied is power. This time I'll add a final important point: Creating wealth requires you to take action.

If few people learn the basics of creating wealth, even fewer will ever know the Wealth Secrets of high-net-worth individuals. This chapter gives you your bonus Wealth Secret, consisting of high-net-worth strategies. I'll introduce you to some of the tactics that can help you to keep more of your hard-earned money for yourself rather than paying more than your fair share to the government, and to invest in ways that can increase greater returns.

High-net-worth individuals enjoy benefits that are inaccessible to the average Jane. These people are courted by private bankers and financial managers who often require a minimum investment of $100,000 or more and can get their clients in on unique investment opportunities with the potential for lucrative returns. They also enjoy tax breaks and benefits. (Don't worry – you can start applying some of this now.)

The "high" in high net worth is relative, of course, but for the purposes of personal finance, it's generally defined as someone with at least $1 million in liquid assets. If that number sounds out of reach to you, remember that wealth is a process. It's a result of practicing a wealth mindset, proven strategy, and consistent execution. Around 6% of US households qualify as high net worth, but there's no reason we can't increase that number and make sure it includes more women like you.[16, 17]

Purse story: Real estate success

Kimberley Nixon is one of the women shifting that statistic in the right direction. When she was growing up, her father worked as a contractor and her mother as a nurse. She watched them both work extremely hard, each of them sometimes working two or more jobs at a time. However, Kimberley's parents gradually turned their W-2 income into investment income. They saved money from their jobs to buy their first home – a fixer-upper, which Kim's father renovated. He also put a hammer in her hand and taught her how to invest some sweat equity in the property.

As she got older, Kimberley watched her parents do this again and again, creating pockets of opportunity for themselves with real estate. Kimberley learned about the process, and she learned to value the assets they created. She was exposed to real estate investing early and often.

16. E Duffin, *Number of households in the U.S. from 1960 to 2022* (statista, 12 December 2022), www.statista.com/statistics/183635/number-of -households-in-the-us, accessed April 25, 2023
17. J Iqbal, *Wealth Segments in the U.S. – At a Glance* (LIMRA Secure Retirement Institute, 2019), https://advisor.johnhancockinsurance .com/content/dam/JHINS/images/NLI/Home%20Log%20Out /Life%20Insurance/Collateral/large-case/day-2/2019_sri_wealth _segments.pdf, accessed April 7, 2023

Because her parents were investors, Kimberley developed a high tolerance for risk by the time she was in a position to invest her own money. However, high tolerance didn't mean she was reckless. She understood that any kind of investment carries risk, but she was willing to step out of her W-2 comfort zone to pursue her wealth goals, always doing her research and making sure she knew the numbers.

"There's this exercise that has to happen, at least for me, where I walk myself through all the risk scenarios, and then what are my two to three ways of de-risking?" Kimberley said. "What are my mitigations? What are my exit opportunities?"

When you go into anything new, it feels scary, Kimberly explained, and she continues to figure out her mitigation strategies to lessen that fear and take action. Kimberley asks herself whether she can afford to lose this money, and what risk any investment poses to her, her family, and her lifestyle. She looks at whether an investment is priced at a point that will allow her to weather some ups and downs, and she considers how long it will be until she needs to access the money.

Pull together

At an early age, Kimberley also learned the value of community in creating wealth. Her parents worked multiple jobs, so various aunts, uncles, and cousins pitched in to help with family and school obligations.

The family is Caribbean, and one custom of their community is to contribute to a communal pot of money in an informal credit-and-loan program, called a susu, that benefits the group. About twenty people would contribute to the susu, and the money would be distributed according to need or to a fixed schedule. These funds functioned like a zero-interest loan for the investors.

Kimberley took that mindset with her to her job at Under Armour. There she joined a Black employee network and immediately set out to make sure her colleagues had the right tools and environment to discuss money and investments. "I wanted to make sure money wasn't taboo in my communities and in my groups of friends," she said. "It's something we can talk about freely."

Whether they were seeking information about how to buy property, improve credit scores, or find the right daycare facility, that trust and information was key to the beginnings of legacy and wealth building.

When I met Kimberley, she had a significant real estate portfolio and a lot of curiosity about investing. She wanted to diversify and to think more in terms of abundance. "I was not diversified at all, and I knew it," Kimberley said. "And I was getting to the point in my career where I also understood that I would need to start looking at investing more broadly and use a skill set that I have, beyond real estate, to make sure that I was building for myself and for my family."

Kimberley admits she was uncomfortable investing in the stock market, in part because she graduated right after a downturn and was in business school during a market crash, and in part simply because it was unfamiliar. Kimberley decided to work with me to get the knowledge she needed about investing in the stock market. We got to work, and Kimberley soon learned how to set up systems and do research. It wasn't long before she was ready for a higher level of investing.

Kimberley already knew how to offset taxable income through real estate investing, and she was taking advantage of those opportunities. However, there were lots of other high-net-worth strategies she needed to consider. Let's take a look at some of the strategies employed by the wealthiest people.

Real estate investing

Kimberley considers herself a "buy and hold" investor when it comes to real estate. This attitude is helpful because it generally takes her about two years to get each property to where she wants it to be. "I rarely let go of properties. I buy well so I do not have to let go," said Kimberley. She spends those first two years putting her support and systems in place, including licensing, property management, repairs and maintenance, attracting the right tenants, and communicating with those tenants. She also makes sure each property is tax-efficient.

Just as Kimberley has done, many high-net-worth individuals often take advantage of several options in the world of real estate. The first one most people think of is rental properties, which are often a good long-term option. With rentals, you not only collect rent, but you can also claim deductions when parts of the property depreciate in value. Assuming you hold on to the property, you'll also have an asset that appreciates over time.

Another option is to purchase a multi-family house and live in one of the units while renting out the others, giving you a rent-free option for your own housing. You can claim expenses such as roof replacement, a new water heater, or landscaping as tax deductions. If you've ever had to handle that kind of upkeep for your home, you know these expenses can reach five figures, so the tax deduction can be significant.

The standard fix-and-flip has become well known as an investment strategy thanks to a plethora of television shows that follow home flippers. As you've probably seen, the process is relatively simple on the surface. You purchase a property at a good price, make improvements, and then sell the property for a profit. Of course, home flipping is more involved than it looks on a thirty-minute show, but it's still a viable real estate investment option. Understand, however, that this real estate strategy has greater tax implications because, in most cases, your profit will be taxed as ordinary income (if you own the property for less than a year). Keep that in mind when you're running the numbers. A $50,000 profit doesn't look so appealing after a 37% tax hit.

Some real estate investors avoid this higher tax rate by holding on to a flip for a few years. In this case, you can rent out the property or live in it before you flip it. This is a great option if you don't mind managing renters, paying a property manager, or moving every few years, during which time you can chip away at improvements.

Here's how it works under current tax law at the time of writing. (Always do your research – tax laws are subject to change.) If you've *owned and occupied* a property for a minimum of two of the last five years, you can avoid capital gains tax on up to $250,000 if you file income taxes as single, and up to $500,000 if you file jointly. This is a great tax shelter. Just remember the house needs to be your primary residence – this exemption doesn't apply to second homes.

As an alternative to living in the home, many flippers take advantage of a like-kind exchange, also called a 1031 exchange. The investor takes the profit from the sale of one investment property and uses it to purchase a like-kind property. Capital gains taxes are deferred because any profit is rolled into the new property.

There are various real estate investment opportunities that don't require you to be a landlord or a flipper, both of which can be time consuming. One way to invest is through a real estate limited partnership (RELP). In this scenario, a group of investors comes together to buy and sell properties in a private investment fund. A general manager handles the ongoing responsibilities of property management. As a limited partner, you enjoy the returns as well as the benefit of writing off some of the property's depreciation, based on the percentage of the investment you own.

When you're ready, there's much more to explore in the world of real estate investing. There are opportunities to create significant tax savings and investment returns, but of course – like any kind of investing – real estate is not without risk. If you decide to explore this area, follow Kimberley's example. Study the market, talk to professionals, and do the numbers.

Opportunity levers

Kimberley is a model of working the opportunity levers available to high-net-worth individuals. Beyond her real estate portfolio, she started a venture fund with a partner and later became a solo general partner. Keep in mind that at the end of 2021, only 14.3% of venture checkwriters were women,[18] and in 2020 just 3% of

---

18. "All Raise VC Checkwriter Dashboard Powered by Crunchbase" (All Raise, June 2021), https://allraise-data-dashboard.s3-us-west -2.amazonaws.com/center/html/index.html, accessed April 7, 2023

venture capital investment partners were Black.[19] This was a bold move into a new arena, and Kimberley brought the same attention to detail and analytical skill that she uses in real estate to the venture fund. "We want to make sure that we don't get to the end of the road, and we fall in love with the founder, and we haven't really done our due diligence on why it's a good investment," said Kimberley.

With this fund, Kimberley is taking advantage of a new opportunity lever. In addition to my work at WealthyU, I also coach women like Kimberley in my twelve-month Legacy Wealth Accelerator, and I encourage them to take advantage of opportunity levers at higher and higher levels. I designed the program as a place where high earners, who already have a handle on the fundamentals of wealth, can learn high-net-worth strategies.

One of our go-to documents is my High-Net-Worth Pyramid. This is a visual depiction of financial strategies that build wealth, with the strategies represented by levels of a pyramid. Each level comprises various opportunity levers.

---

19. B Coombs, "Black-led VC fund aims to even the playing field for minority health-tech startups" (CNBC, February 16, 2022), www .cnbc.com/2022/02/15/black-led-vc-fund-aims-to-even-the-playing -field-for-minority-health-tech-start-ups-.html, accessed April 7, 2023

High-Net-Worth investment strategies

The High-Net-Worth Pyramid offers strategies you can look forward to implementing in the future as your wealth grows and you have more assets to invest. Understand that few people will ever have the ability to utilize most of those opportunity levers because they won't do the foundational wealth work you started in the early chapters of this book. If you're feeling behind, shift your mindset – you're already ahead of the pack.

Tax prep vs tax planning

Every year, from early January to mid-April, the airwaves are filled with ads from tax preparers who want to prepare and file your taxes for you. Of course, it's wise to have a professional do that job. However, high-net-worth individuals understand that taxes are something to think about year-round, not just as we approach April 15th every year.

Tax planning means you consult with professionals to develop the strategies that will best help you keep more of what you make and invest more in your portfolio. As you grow your wealth, you'll need to keep in touch with your tax strategist to determine not only what you might owe or whether you need to make an estimated payment, but also to discuss strategies to minimize your tax liability.

Have you ever wondered how the wealthiest people pay so little in taxes, while the little guys seem to carry more than their fair share of the load? It's because the wealthy understand tax law and use it to their advantage.

Advantages of entrepreneurship

Here's the best-kept open secret about wealth building: Earned income is taxed at a higher rate than all other income. It's important for you to understand the implications of that fact and to be clear about how it's limiting your ability to build wealth. Most people go to work every day, get their paycheck every two weeks, and assume the amount of tax on their salary is just the way it is. They never consider that there may be ways to earn income and pay significantly less tax on it.

We've already discussed the idea of finding your super-power and turning your skill set into an asset. When you use those skills to start a business, not only can you earn more income, but you can also access more tax advantages. Most of us were trained to be earners, not owners, but the government rewards entrepreneurship. It does so by offering incentives in the tax law. For instance, you can deduct all kinds of expenses related to your business, from education and training expenses and travel to the equipment you need and the salary you pay yourself.

LLC and S-Corp

From almost the first page of *Wealth Secrets*, I've encouraged you to consider a side business or a full-time business as a wealth-building strategy. Going into business for yourself is an important step because it provides you with another income stream, but just becoming an entrepreneur isn't enough. You might start off as a sole proprietor, recognized as the single owner of your business entity. In that case, the business profits are exclusively yours and are considered pass-through income. This typically means you'll pay more in taxes than other business designations because your profits are taxed at your personal income rate. As a sole proprietor, your personal assets can be seized to collect on business debt or in the event that your business is on the losing end of a lawsuit, giving you less asset protection than if you register your business as an LLC.

Instead of running your business as a sole proprietorship, I recommend you form an LLC as soon as you can, even if you're your only employee. You can file the paperwork on your own, through a legal service or with an attorney. Follow your state's guidelines, typically found through your Secretary of State, to ensure you're in compliance with requirements for licenses, permits, and local taxes.

When you file taxes as a sole proprietor, you file under your own social security number. When you register your business as an LLC, you'll have a tax ID number for your business, and more importantly, a measure of legal protection for your personal assets. LLC stands for limited liability corporation, so named because it limits your personal liability in the event of collection attempts on business debt or a lawsuit against your business. These are very real risks in every industry – some more than others – so it's worth the time and small investment to form an LLC. Keep in mind, however, that with an LLC, your profits are still considered pass-through income for tax purposes.

As your profits increase, you can file Form 2553 with the IRS, which allows you to file your business taxes as an S-Corp even when your business is still registered as an LLC. While most small businesses won't need to register as an S-Corp, the S-Corp designation for tax purposes can save you a lot of money. At the time of writing, the net profit on an LLC's Schedule C is subject to 15.3% self-employment tax in addition to federal liability. The profit of an S-Corp is not. When you file your business taxes as an S-Corp, you must pay yourself a salary as an employee of your business. Talk to your tax professional to find out when you should change your filing and at what point it makes sense to pay yourself a salary rather than an owner's draw.

SEP-IRA

The idea behind tax advantages in retirement portfolios is that you'll be in a lower tax bracket when it comes time to use that money and pay taxes on your withdrawals. A SEP-IRA – a simplified employee pension individual retirement arrangement – allows business owners to contribute to a retirement plan for themselves and for any employees. Contributions follow the same rules for contributions and deductions as any other IRAs.

If you're running a business while working a job, you can contribute to both a SEP-IRA and your company's retirement plan. This is a great way to take advantage of multiple benefits. You can get the matching contribution from your employer while also leveraging your tax advantages in your business.

In the SEP, you can contribute up to 25% of your net earnings up to $66,000 (as of 2023). The contribution is a dollar-for-dollar deduction within your company, meaning it's deducted from your taxable income. For example, if your net profit is $200,000, you could contribute $50,000 to your SEP, resulting in taxable income of $150,000 on your Schedule C. You save on taxes and your retirement portfolio grows.

Additional strategies

There are a lot of other high-net-worth strategies to consider. These include deferred compensation, in which your employer sets aside money that you can access when you retire. This allows you to file at a lower tax bracket and minimize your tax liability. High-net-worth individuals often create a charitable trust. This would require you to establish a nonprofit organization and put money into the trust, which then gives you a dollar-for-dollar deduction when you file your income taxes.

There's also a backdoor Roth IRA. In that scenario, you open a standard IRA and then convert it later to a Roth IRA. This gives you flexibility with income and contribution limits. A financial advisor such as a wealth coach or a financial planner can help you determine if and when these accounts are right for you.

While you might not yet be close to qualifying as a high-net-worth individual, some of these strategies are already available to you and can help you get there. We cover a lot more ground in my Legacy Wealth Accelerator group, but at this point you can understand that there are a lot of ways for you to build wealth and to save on taxes, and those opportunities grow with your net worth. Remember, your worth isn't determined solely by what you earn, but also by what you do with those earnings.

What an advantage Kimberley had, as she grew up observing parents who learned how to invest in real estate and not only executed on that knowledge but also brought her into the business at an early age. While you might not have had the same opportunity in your childhood, you have it now, and you can pass it on to the next generation in your family or through mentorship, just as Kimberley did for her coworkers.

Find a community of women who are making these kinds of wealth-building moves and learn from them. In the next chapter, we'll talk about exactly how you can get in the room, on the course, or wherever those women are, then learn from them and benefit from those relationships.

11
Bonus Wealth Secret: Build Social Capital

I f you consistently apply all the Wealth Secrets I've shared with you so far – including the high-net-worth strategies – the odds that you'll get wealthy, which might have once seemed stacked against you, will be heavily in your favor. You'll greatly increase your chances of growing your net worth over time and eventually reaching your wealth goals. However, there's a final bonus Wealth Secret that can amplify your wealth-building power and help you reach your financial goals faster. It's simple: *Your network drives your net worth.*

So far, we've focused on developing a wealth mindset, investing in yourself, and investing your money for growth. Those things will always be essential. They're critical factors in how you grow your net worth. However, it's just as important that you invest in people and relationships to build your social capital – no one succeeds at anything alone. Whether you're growing your business, looking to jump up the corporate ladder, or on the lookout for your next investment opportunity, the people you know – and who know you – can make all the difference. In most cases, your financial condition will come to mirror that of the people you spend the most time with, so it's important to be deliberate and discerning in building your network.

Purse story: Joining the game

Growing up in Baltimore, Maryland, WealthyU member Jandie Turner always had a love of sports. She grew up playing softball and basketball, and after studying engineering at the University of Virginia, she built a career in management consulting. One of her husband's personal passions incidentally led Jandie to her most effective networking strategy and a new career.

One Saturday afternoon, Jandie's husband was watching the LPGA on television, and the women were playing a Skins game. "They were winning money for their charities," explained Jandie. "So if you win this hole, you get $10,000. You win the next one, you get $10,000." The combination of sports and gambling appealed to Jandie, and as a natural athlete, she thought it looked easy. Excited to try something new, she asked her husband to teach her the game. He agreed, and according to Jandie, his efforts turned out to be an endeavor of love.

"Well, my God!" said Jandie. "Golf is the hardest sport I have ever attempted to learn how to play." Accustomed to sports coming instinctively to her, Jandie was surprised to find golf was different. She felt nervous on the course and shied away from playing with other people, letting group after group go ahead of them. Eventually, her husband told her, "You can't do that. There's always going to be another group."

She was mortified when her husband suggested they play with a couple of guys. Despite her doubts, Jandie finally decided to go all in and play the way the game was supposed to be played, and she discovered she wasn't nearly as bad a golfer as she'd assumed. With that bit of encouragement, she dedicated herself to developing her skills on the golf course, and she soon learned golf was more than a way to pass the time. It was a key that opened doors to new opportunities. It was the game of business.

It's not what you know – it's who you know and who knows you

Rapper and activist Nipsey Hussle said, "If you look at the people in your circle and don't get inspired, then you don't have a circle. You have a cage." Are you the wealthiest or the most accomplished in your friend group and in most rooms where you spend time? Are you usually the only one with the strongest wealth mindset? If so, it's time to meet new people. Yes, your education, the skills you've developed, and your experience matter. They matter a lot. However, if you're isolated and without a strong network, few people will know what you have to offer, and your exposure to new ideas and opportunities will be limited. You want people to think of you when they need an expert in your area or have an opportunity that could make a difference to your net-worth goals.

You've probably heard the adage "Your network is your net worth." It's absolutely true, and that's good news for you as you apply the Wealth Secrets, because your network is something you can control. Even as you read this, you might be only one phone call, one meeting, or one game of golf away from someone who can open new doors for you. You might be just two or three degrees of separation from a strategic business partner, a new client referral, or the connection you need to land a position with your dream company.

Right now, you probably don't have many (or any) billionaire friends. Billionaires tend to hang out with billionaires. However, part of the reason you're not a billionaire is because you're not in their circle. It seems like a Catch-22, but it's actually not. You don't have to make the leap all the way to ten-figure rooms from wherever you are right now. Focus instead on surrounding yourself with people who have a wealth mindset, who are connected to your potential clients or employers, or who have access to people you'd like to get to know. As you invest in those relationships, you'll naturally position yourself in rooms with people whose net worth matches and exceeds your own.

Of course, you can incrementally expand your network to include people with a greater net worth, but that shouldn't be your only criterion. The wealthy surround themselves with smart people, people in leadership positions, and influential experts. Your network should include contacts who have a body of knowledge different from your own, work in industries you might want to explore, or have influence in your industry or community. They may not all be at the seven-figure mark or higher, but the mayor of your city, the president of a university, or a consultant whose offerings complement yours can all add value to your network.

One of the most effective ways to get wealthy is to put yourself in the spaces where wealthy people work and play. Think about how the people in your circles talk about money. Do they talk in terms of scarcity and never having enough? If they're doing well financially, are they still afraid the good times won't last or a recession will wipe out all they've earned? Contrast that with what you know about wealthy people. They are prudent with their finances but not fearful. They look at a downturn as a chance to increase their wealth. Rather than relying solely on experts to tell them what to do, they're willing to learn what it takes to maximize their assets.

If you spend a lot of time with the first group, how do you suppose you'll approach financial decisions? Now picture yourself engaged with the second group. Can you feel the difference? Business deals often happen because of a personal connection. Make those connections and allow people in your growing network to observe your character and your unique abilities.

Consider golf

Golf has long been recognized as the game where business deals happen. However, many women, especially Black women and other women of color, have felt locked out of the sport. They don't see themselves on the course, and so they feel like they don't belong. Jandie is committed to correcting this misassumption. She pointed out that, although growth of the sport as a whole has leveled off, certain segments of golfers, including women, minorities, and juniors, are growing. In 2011, women made up just 19% of golfers, but by 2021, they had reached 25%.[20] Jandie also made note of a Black women's golf club that's been around since 1938. "So we've been there," she said. "We're waiting

---

20. M Croley, "Long Excluded, Female Golfers Are Now Key Driver of Game's Growth" (Bloomberg UK, March 11, 2022), www.bloomberg .com/news/articles/2022-03-11/long-excluded-female-golfers-are -now-key-driver-of-game-s-growth, accessed April 7, 2023

for everyone else to come to the table to see what's available."

When she joined me on my television program, *Get Wealthy*, to talk about her love of the game and how it has served her, Jandie explained, "You might not be interested in playing golf, but your colleagues are. Your customers are. Your suppliers are."

Jandie considers golf a career accelerant, and she painted a clear picture as to why that can be the case. "If you work in an organization where your boss or your boss two levels up is a golfer, nine times out of ten there will be plenty of business opportunities to represent that organization in a charity golf tournament or to attend a golf tournament. And if your name pops up on [their] list as a golfer, it's fantastic. Otherwise, on Friday afternoon, you're sitting at your desk, and those who do play golf are out building relationships with the boss or their peers and having their name in the conversation."

Jandie was so impressed by the value of golf, she wrote her first book, *Golf: The Sport of Business*, to introduce the game and its many benefits to more people.[21] Even if you don't want to play golf or are physically unable to, according to Jandie, there are still plenty of opportunities for you to be around the game. Attend professional golf events and invite a prospective client or someone

---

21. J Smith Turner, *Golf: The Sport of Business* (2014)

else you want to get to know better in your professional life. A golf tournament, Jandie pointed out, isn't like most sporting events. "It's an opportunity to see the beauty of the golf course and walk the course with the golfers. It's also an opportunity to sit in a chalet over one of the signature holes and sip wine and have decent, quiet conversation."

Jandie went on to say, "One of the things that I've learned from producing hundreds, if not thousands, of golf tournaments is that business gets done on the golf course. The conversations are a bit different. The relationships are a bit more authentic. So when you think about your network, who plays golf? For me, [those are] the people I want in my network."

Early on, as she dabbled in the sport and met other women who also wanted to play, Jandie organized her first tournament, a small event of sixteen women, and she hit up her corporate connections to donate swag and prizes. The women had a great time, and the tournament was a success, but it was the after-tournament activities that Jandie realized were most powerful. The women didn't want to go home right away, and they gathered in the clubhouse to talk and get to know each other better. They also asked when the next tournament would be, and Jandie scrambled to organize another one a couple of months later.

Soon, she was running more and more events, and then she ran an analysis of the golf industry. She also learned in her research that golf was all about networking, corporate partnerships, and corporate sponsorships. Along with her event management company, Acuity Events, she launched Acuity Sports, a company focused on helping nonprofits host golf tournaments as fund-raising events.

Jandie produces corporate golf and spa retreats and consistently sees the advantage that women have when they mix in some golf. "Invariably the women head to the spa and the men head over to the golf course," she said, "and the one or two women who go to the golf course, trust me, they stand out. Their name is in the conversation, and they get recognized. So again, you want your name and yourself to be in the conversation."

Jandie offered some tips for people who are new to the game:

1. **Learn the basics:** Start by taking at least five lessons. Keep in mind that you can borrow clubs from the course or the facility before you invest in your own. Jandie highly recommends you practice between lessons to make sure what you learn sticks and you get your money's worth.

2. **Learn the rules:** "Good golfers don't mind playing with bad golfers or a not-so-good golfer," said Jandie. "But they do mind playing with people who are slow and people who don't know the rules." She encourages people to learn

one or two rules a day, which means you'll cover most of the rules within a month.

3. **Follow convention:** The game of golf has its own etiquette, which is nearly as important as the rules themselves – things like how to dress and how to proceed on the court. She suggests you take the time to familiarize yourself with that etiquette as well. As you ease into golf and spend more time on the course, you can look into buying your own clubs (used are fine) and appropriate clothes.

4. **Pick your locations:** You might consider joining a club or signing up to play in a league. A league is a good way to get consistent practice as well as meet people, as the group of fifteen or twenty players usually gets mixed up each week. Jandie suggests you also check with your employer to see whether they have company golf clinics or participate in a league.

In Jandie's experience, a golf outing is much better than a lunch appointment. "Let's face it, if you invite me to lunch for business, I'm going to be on my best behavior for that hour," she said. However, golf, which takes place in a relaxed setting with minimal distractions, provides a different environment, which can open up communication in unique ways. Not to mention the insights a round can give you into someone's personality.

"On the golf course, you're going to see the good, the bad, and the ugly," Jandie said. "You're going to see me hit great shots, and you're going to see me hit downright ugly shots. But what matters and what you can infer from seeing that is how do I handle that?"

Golf provides an opportunity to read people. Are they strutting around and bragging on the good shots? Are they tossing clubs and sulking on the bad shots? A lot happens between hitting the shots, which accounts for a minuscule portion of the time on a course. Take note of your fellow players' habits and behaviors. Does the other person show up on time? How do they treat their partners? What kind of risks do they take? Additionally, a round of golf provides a chance to find common ground and to allow others to get some insight into your character.

"So if I were entering into a business partnership with somebody, I would take them out on the golf course," Jandie said. "And perhaps even if you were entering into a marriage or relationship, because how they show up on the golf course is nine times out of ten how they show up in life."

Time spent playing golf together is great for building rapport and learning more about people and their needs. You don't want to jump right into a sales pitch, of course. Instead, take the time to get to know the people you connect with through golf. Jandie suggests reading their mood and the situation to decide whether an after-round drink or dinner is a place to bring up business, or whether it's more appropriate to follow up later with an email or phone call.

Success is a contact sport

Meeting people, collecting business cards, or creating thousands of connections on LinkedIn isn't enough to build true social capital. Effective networking demands that you take the initiative and nurture those relationships, and that requires staying in contact. It's important to interact with the people in your network on a regular basis to ensure you're top of mind when they need someone who does what you do or when they have an investment opportunity they want to discuss.

Maintaining your network doesn't have to be difficult or time consuming, and it can be enjoyable. If you belong to an organization, such as a women's or co-ed golf league, a professional networking group, an alumni association, or a service organization that attracts the kind of people you want in your network, you have ample opportunity to maintain consistent contact with other members. Of course, that means you need to show up for meetings and events. Allow people to see you adding value, if only with your presence, insightful questions, and helpful suggestions, and don't be afraid to put yourself forward for leadership positions.

It's wise to have a balance of online and offline contacts. Platforms like LinkedIn, mastermind groups that meet online, and even coworking groups allow you to connect with people all over the country and the world. The women of WealthyU may never interact in the real world – although many of them do – but they're able to connect and support each other in very real ways. However, your online networking should be balanced with real-world connections. If you're just beginning to develop your network in your area, check your local chambers of commerce, industry organizations, and small-business groups.

One of the most effective ways to maintain relationships with your growing list of connections is to create a system to follow up with people. For instance, you might maintain a spreadsheet or find simple contact-management software to keep track of your contacts and how you're interacting with them. Contact one to three people a day. Share an article or book recommendation you think will make a difference for them. Ask how you can help them achieve their goals. Connect two people who should know each other. Acknowledge birthdays and anniversaries. Give before you seek to take; and use your best judgment to decide when it makes sense to ask for help such as an introduction to someone they know well, a client referral, or a recommendation for a job.

Whether you're networking through a golf game or some other avenue, it's important to have the right mindset. Your network will drive your net worth, but it will only drive it in the right direction if you network with a clear strategy and consistent execution. Your next great wealth opportunity could be just one connection away. It's up to you to make sure that connection happens. Jandie did it, and she has continued to do it over and over again. You can do it too.

12
Make The Shift To Wealth

So far in this book, you've met women who gave us great insight into the Wealth Secrets, including Xina Eilands's approach to systems and Diya Winn's mastery of financial fundamentals. In this final chapter, I'd like to introduce a woman who has used *all* the Wealth Secrets to create a total financial transformation in her life.

Purse story: Surpassing all expectations

Leigha Armstrong is our final example of a WealthyU woman who made the most of the strategies she learned in the program, and she did it while making up for lost time as well as starting her life anew, after suffering a tragic loss during the pandemic. At fifty years old, Leigha had already taken the first small steps toward changing her financial picture, when her life was upended by an unexpected turn of events. In July 2020 her fiancé lost his life to COVID-19. Rather than allow his unexpected passing to derail her, however, Leigha made a decision to use it as the inspiration to create a better financial future for herself.

"I decided to put that energy from grieving into making a change for the better," Leigha said. "And I had decided that, in honoring his memory, he was always about enjoying life and making good decisions about the future, and so somehow, I had to get the knowledge that I needed to carry forward and to plan my life."

Leigha started where all my WealthyU clients begin, by shifting her mindset. Like a lot of people, she'd witnessed debt being misused as she was growing up. She had a good family life, but financial knowledge was nowhere in the mix. Her parents carried balances from month to month and considered large purchases only in terms of how much they'd have to pay each month. Leigha doesn't fault them, however. After all, no one had passed along wealth principles to her parents either, and money was tight in part because they wanted to send Leigha to good schools. On postal service salaries, they paid private school tuition for her in the high-priced state of California. It made sense at the time, since education has long been considered the ticket to success for middle-class families. Many parents have taken on debt to give their children those opportunities.

As a young adult, Leigha adopted the same mindset as her parents and made purchasing decisions based on monthly payments. She also allowed herself to splurge on what many would consider luxuries, because she felt she could afford them. However, in her mid-thirties, Leigha started to make a shift. She still carried balances and had what she'd learned to consider bad debt, but she no longer made purchasing decisions based on monthly payments.

Leigha knew she wanted to make a change, but she wasn't sure how to do it. She decided to research the matter on her own and immersed herself in reading books on personal finance. One day she caught my television program, *Wealth Secrets*, and she signed up to receive my newsletter. After she decided to take the plunge and join WealthyU, Leigha took me up on the challenge to find money in her existing budget – and she found a pretty good amount.

"I'll never forget," Leigha said, "that week I found $700 in my budget that I was essentially just wasting – subscriptions, excessive hair appointments, excessive nail appointments – just all kinds of stuff that, honestly, I did because I could. It's okay to enjoy things, but you really have to put up boundaries for yourself. I found $700 that week. And so that was motivating for me."

The following month, Leigha exercised some stock options that were maturing, and she wiped out her credit card debt. The month after that, she paid off her car. Those two moves freed up even more of her cash. "And lo and behold, I had $2,500 in my budget that I could invest – that I could do the right thing with," she said. "It just felt so good. It was the first time in my life that I was debt-free, except my home. It was just the most exuberant feeling that I've ever felt. And so that was motivating [to me] to learn more."

Leigha was well on her way to creating and executing a goal-focused action. You may recall that Tamika Smith, who you met in Chapter 6, followed a similar path, finding pockets of money and figuring out how to disperse it. Tamika also trimmed her excess spending and paid off her debts one by one, in a deliberate fashion, and found herself with a sizable amount she could direct into her retirement portfolio. She too enjoyed the feeling that came with freedom from debt.

That exuberant feeling Leigha and Tamika described is exactly how you'll feel once you embrace wealth building and incorporate the Wealth Secrets into your life. Here's how Leigha put all the Wealth Secrets together.

1. **Focus on increasing your net worth:** Leigha set boundaries on her spending and wiped out her debt to free up funds she could use to increase her investment portfolio.

2. **Find your superpower:** Leigha parlayed her skills and experience into a new job, which doubled her salary.

3. **Increase your financial acumen:** Leigha redirected some of her discretionary income from frivolous spending into vehicles that would produce greater returns for her.

4. **Develop a goal-focused action plan:** Leigha took a hard look at her finances and got clear about her numbers. Then she made a detailed plan and followed through on it.

5. **Recognize problems as opportunities:** Leigha increased her contribution to her 401(k), adjusted the mix to a more aggressive one, and added more stocks to her portfolio.

6. **Leverage tech and systems:** Leigha automated her contributions to her retirement portfolio, signed up for the Stash app to leverage technology, and set her saving and investing plans on autopilot.

7. **Protect what you build:** Leigha is paving the way for others to see what she's accomplished and to model their financial futures after hers. As she shares her story, she inspires more women to take similar action.

Leigha learned how to do all these things, and even though she's had quite a bit of success, she knows she's only just begun. That's because her mindset has changed and she finally recognizes the possibilities. When she first found the $700 in her budget, she went into action. She dove into the stock analysis workshop in WealthyU, and she used the knowledge she gained to pick three stocks and a mutual fund for her Stash account. They included pharmaceutical company Moderna, Walmart, and Apple, plus a mutual fund with blue-chip companies that offered high dividends. Leigha also set up her Stash account to invest automatically so she could take advantage of dollar-cost averaging – systematic investing that can lessen the impact an investor experiences when the market takes a downturn – rather than trying to time the market.

"I was amazed at how much I didn't miss the money," she said. "I had it coming out of my discretionary account, so it was in there with the hair-appointment money and all the money I had allocated for different stuff. And over time, I started increasing the [automatic] contribution to those stocks."

Leigha also increased the contribution to her 401(k), and she reevaluated how aggressive she was (or wasn't) being with her 401(k) mutual funds. She mixed things up to improve on her returns.

Leigha credits two big shifts for her success. First, she made a mindset shift, so she doesn't tolerate carrying balances anymore. Leigha said she saw paying off her debt like a game of Whac-a-Mole. As soon as she needs to use her credit card, such as when she checks into a hotel or rents a car, and then sees a balance, she whacks it by paying it off. Second, she had the necessary strategy to dive into investing via Stash with automatic investments.

Leigha said she had an epiphany during a WealthyU challenge, in the summer of 2020, when I asked her group whether they were serving other people's goals with their money or whether their money was serving their own goals. "It was a profound statement for me, because it's the day I woke up and realized – all the spending I'm doing, I'm serving other people's goals for their business, for sales for them, without a strategy to serve myself," she said. "Not just now, but like wanting to retire in a few years. What am I doing? And so I kind of adopted that as my mantra when I looked through the lens of things that I want."

A year and a half after she joined WealthyU, Leigha moved back west to be closer to her parents. She credits getting her financial house in order for her ability to make the move and find and buy a house in a super-hot market. She got an excellent rate on a mortgage because she had a great credit score – an 849, in fact, putting her in the top 2% of the population – and she was able to make a sizable down payment from the sale of her house in Georgia.[22] She also had cash on hand

---

22. C DeVon, "People with perfect credit scores have 3 key traits in common, Experian reports" (CNBC, December 2, 2022), www.cnbc.com/2022/12/02/experian-people-with-perfect-credit-scores-have-3-things-in-common.html, accessed April 7, 2023

to deal with any number of expenses that arose with a long-distance move and a new house.

"I took a snapshot of my credit score a few months ago and sent it to a friend," Leigha said. "I [explained] 'I've never been in this area.' I had an 849; that is because of not tolerating that debt." Leigha's example illustrates the power we have when we're in good financial standing and the way we can leverage opportunities when we position ourselves for wealth.

As you can see, Leigha made a complete transformation in her finances and is well on her way to living a wealthy lifestyle. You can do the same. As you employ each of the seven Wealth Secrets, remember you also have the two bonus ones – employing high-net-worth strategies and building your social capital – in your toolbox too. You don't have to hit seven figures in liquid assets to begin to make those Wealth Secrets work for you. Start where you are, with what you have.

Conclusion

I f you're like most of my clients and the women I meet at conferences, seminars, and social events, you're pursuing wealth for a number of reasons. Perhaps you want to make sure your children can get through college without taking on debt. Maybe you want to pay off your own student loans, simultaneously save for retirement, and enjoy a comfortable life in the short-term. Or maybe you have a big vision of shifting the status quo in your community. You might even want all these things and more. The women you've met in these pages – women just like you – have accomplished all those goals and more. Now that you've discovered the secrets of the wealthy, you can achieve similar goals.

You've embarked on what will be a lifelong journey. The key to completing it successfully is to remain consistent in expanding your knowledge, and staying abreast of the latest trends and what's going on in the markets, so you can respond rather than react.

When you realize you can take control of your financial future and you start to rack up the wins, you'll want to keep it going. Most women who go through this process discover they come to love the challenge of finding new opportunities to put their money to work for them.

I want you to join me, the women you've met here, and the women in my programs in my mission to close the wealth gap. Unfortunately, women are only half as likely to invest in the stock market as men are.[23] However, we have the power to change this. It starts with basic financial education and tools and continues with the Wealth Secrets being implemented by women like you and then passed on to future generations.

Wealthy women have a unique view on money and develop patterns of behavior to take charge of their net worth. They ask themselves what the best use of their money is and how they can make their money make more money. Wealthy women take the time to master financial fundamentals, and they commit to being lifetime learners. These are habits you've started to

---

23. M Mitra, "Women Are Handling Stock Market Volatility Way Better Than Men" (Money Group, September 23, 2022), https://money.com /stock-market-volatility-women-vs-men, accessed April 7, 2023

build. As your knowledge grows, so will your ability to discern good information from bad.

As you learn more about how money works, you might decide to attend stockholder meetings. You'll be able to hold your advisors accountable, and if a professional is unable to clearly explain a concept or product, you'll have the confidence to make your own decision and discontinue the relationship if necessary.

You now know how to pay yourself first and through automatic savings accounts and investment programs that let you invest in stocks and mutual funds. You recognize the importance of maintaining your emergency fund. You'll never have to guess at your financial picture, because you'll have your figures close at hand and top of mind, and you'll stay focused on your long-term goals.

Sophonia Hardaway (in Chapter 7) also embraced the idea of diversifying her assets. As she grew up, she saw diversification in action as she watched the various ways her family brought in income, and she applied that thinking to her money skills. Sophonia rented out her townhouse, bought different insurance products, purchased a franchise, and learned how to balance risk and reward.

Both Sophonia and Leigha (Chapter 12), along with the other WealthyU students you've met in this book, took the time to educate themselves about their portfolios.

They learned how to discuss their options with financial advisors and how to take control of their own futures.

Reading this book and recognizing your circumstances in the stories I've shared is the start of developing your wealth mindset. All the strategies you need are laid out for you. Now it's up to you to execute. There's never been a better time or more opportunities available to grow your money and take control of your financial future.

I believe wholeheartedly in your ability to get wealthy. I've watched so many women come from feeling behind to catching up and surpassing where they'd ever dreamed they could be with their money. It's not as complicated as the old-school experts would have you believe, and contrary to what we've been taught, there are no limits to the wealth you can create. The opportunity levers available to you are unique to your life. Take advantage of them and create the wealth you deserve.

Acknowledgments

A special thank you to Candice Davis for her editing and copywriting skills and unwavering support for this project.

The Author

Deborah Owens, America's Wealth Coach™, is on a mission to help women, through coaching, accountability, and support, overcome their fear of investing. A twenty-year financial services industry veteran and former vice president with Fidelity Investments, she makes the information once reserved for high-net-worth clients of private wealth managers accessible to women at every income level. Deborah is the founder of WealthyU, a financial wellness company, which has a proven track record of helping thousands of women transform from cautious savers into confident investors. She holds a Master of Business Administration from Loyola University of Maryland.

For more information:

⊕ www.WealthyU.com
🅕 www.facebook.com/DeborahOwensPage
🅛 www.linkedin.com/in/deborahowens
🅧 https://twitter.com/deborahowens
🅞 www.instagram.com/iamdeborahowens